Yes!
It All Began
with Love

Jim Waters

WESTBOW
PRESS®
A DIVISION OF THOMAS NELSON
& ZONDERVAN

Unless otherwise indicated, Scripture taken from the HOLY BIBLE,
NEW INTERNATIONAL VERSION® NIV®. Copyright © 1973, 1978,
1984, 2011 by Biblica, Inc.® Used by permission of Biblica, Inc.®

WestBow Press books may be ordered through booksellers or by contacting:

WestBow Press
A Division of Thomas Nelson & Zondervan
1663 Liberty Drive
Bloomington, IN 47403
www.westbowpress.com
1 (866) 928-1240

ISBN: 978-1-5127-7407-8 (sc)
ISBN: 978-1-5127-7408-5 (hc)
ISBN: 978-1-5127-7406-1 (e)

Library of Congress Control Number: 2017901417

Print information available on the last page.

WestBow Press rev. date: 02/06/2017

Contents

Preface

Today I'm in front of my computer with a repaired heart and an excited, enlivened spirit. It's been six weeks since my open-heart surgery—a time the Lord used to focus me on the crux and running theme of this work. Refreshed and rejuvenated in body, mind, and spirit, I am very thankful. As always, God has neither left me nor forsaken me.

During my time of infirmity, the Lord has brought to me a clear sense of what he desires I convey regarding the Christian's daily fellowship with the Holy Spirit. Through his Word, highlights of insight concerning his love shared with you and me through the Holy Spirit have illuminated truths set in place since the beginning. Over the years of my Christian life, through his own Word and in the company of believing authors, the Lord has set in place a platform from which I can share.

God's timing is the best timing. I was about forty years old when he brought me to a real awareness of the Holy Spirit. Many hours of study, sermons, and writings opened the door that has swung ever wider while revealing more and more of his eternal purpose and daily activity in the believer.

The main purpose at hand is that I share with you, from the beginning, an obvious truth concerning the Holy Spirit—a truth needed to be seen first and foremost that will put you, the Christian, into a better understanding of his existence. Because of my being down for the count, I have further surrendered to the Lord. Through this time of fresh focus, he has continued to guide me along his intended path. The theme of *Yes! It All Began with Love* was set in motion by no design of my own. It is that which the Lord has shown me.

Come share with me the excitement of the Spirit of the Lord actively living within our individual saved souls as he leads out in love … Yes, eternal daily love.

Friend, it is you I am addressing, I must consider that you may not be well versed when it comes to the subject of the Holy Spirit. I will, on the other hand, take it as fact that you are a Christian redeemed by the salvation of Jesus Christ. *Yes! It All Began with Love* is written for the Christian.

Acknowledgments

I first and foremost give praise to Jesus Christ for the opportunity of conveying this message to you, my Christian brother or sister. It is through his great sacrifice by the will of the Father that you and I and every saved soul now have the Holy Spirit permanently indwelling us. He is our Guide, Counselor, Sanctifier, and Sustainer.

I also thank my wife, Elaine, for continually encouraging me to complete this work so it can be shared with Christians around the world, that the Holy Spirit will become an evident daily part of the believer's life with the Lord.

My thanks go out to all who have been supportive of me through Christian love and prayer. Thank you all!

J. W.

The Holy Spirit's Importance to You as a Christian

Christian,

You made a conscious decision. You accepted Jesus as your Lord and Savior. Through his unconditional sacrifice, he made it possible for you to have forgiveness of your sin and eternal life. This is magnificent!

With this truth refreshed in your memory, in all fairness, are you pleased with your life in the Lord? Do you have joy and peace flowing from within? Do you truly love Jesus, your Savior? Are you consciously aware that he faithfully followed through with a major promise, which you are experiencing right now?

At this moment, Jesus is physically at the right hand of the Father in all his glory. And at this same moment, his Spirit is eternally dwelling within your saved soul, just as he promised. This is cause for great comfort and confidence.

Do you know the Holy Spirit? Have you accepted that he truly lives in your redeemed soul?

The fact is, Jesus loves you so much that he is responsible for the Holy Spirit permanently residing in your soul. Jesus asked the Father

1

to send the Holy Spirit to you. It was through the perfect sacrifice of Jesus's death on the cross and his glorious resurrection from the dead that you have received the magnificent promise of promises—the Holy Spirit. It is through him and his never-ending guidance that you have eternal life with the Lord Jesus.

Christian, if you could place a one-through-ten rating on how important the Holy Spirit is to you, what would it be? Since you said yes to Jesus, have you given the Spirit consideration? Do you acknowledge him daily?

For many Christians, the Holy Spirit is only sparsely acknowledged. The truth is that he *is* reality. He *is* God. Therefore, he plays an equal role with Jesus and the Father. Once actually realized, the Holy Spirit's value in the Christian's life becomes daily reality. For many Christians, a lack of understanding and acknowledgment plays a major part in keeping the Holy Spirit at a distance or completely left out of the picture.

It is because of the above truth and through my own personal experience of not initially giving the Holy Spirit his full place in my life that I am compelled to share with you, through the evidence found in God's Word, the Bible, his everlasting importance in your Christian life.

Over my years as a pastor, I've come to realize many Christians merely acknowledge the Holy Spirit's existence. Sadly, the Spirit of God is left out of the daily scene. This is not God's plan. It is because of the immense love God has for us that he has openly given each of us his Spirit.

Here is your opportunity to knowingly get plugged in and connected. Jesus willingly did the work on the cross for the forgiveness of sin. Through his resurrection from the dead, he lovingly paved the way for you and me to have eternal life with him. It is through the Holy Spirit that he promised you and me that our gift of eternal life is secured; and he—the Holy Spirit—daily works within us that we will realistically enjoy and exercise our salvation.

Christian, the Holy Spirit is your Counselor, Comforter, and Guide. He is your Sanctifier and Sustainer. The moment you received Christ as Lord and Savior, the Holy Spirit entered your saved soul, taking up permanent residence. And from that very moment, he truly began his work in and through you. This is not only exciting news but is also God's will, purpose, and eternal plan for you and every Christian!

Step together with me into this truth while you allow the Holy Spirit to joyfully reveal himself to you through the agape love of the Father displayed to you through Jesus the Lord.

It is through my excitement after a number of years of hands-on research and practical experience that I will now share with you, in book form, the importance of the Holy Spirit in the life of each Christian. I have also come to the serene understanding that all things work in God's timing and to his good purpose, centered in love. The crux of our existence as redeemed ones of Christ rests in the continued daily guidance of the Holy Spirit, which was ushered in through the unconditional sacrifice of Jesus through the will of the Father.

The perfect reason God placed his Spirit in the Christian heart is love. This is so important, yet we tend to overlook the obvious. If an affirmation can be given with all exuberance, it is the simply profound exclamation **"Yes!"**

Out of the depth of his heart, God first said yes when he chose to create us. And from out of the depths of our redeemed souls, it is his desire that we say yes as we accept him as our Creator, Savior, and Sustainer.

Without a doubt, we are loved by him from the core of his everlasting existence! He loves us so much he gave his one and only Son as the perfect sacrifice for the sin that separated us from him. "For we are God's workmanship, created in Christ Jesus to do good works, which God prepared in advance for us to do" (Ephesians 2:10).

It is through the Holy Spirit's guiding that we are equipped to daily do the good works God has prepared for us to do. Unless we have a Guide, we have no positive direction. God would not have created us without a long-term plan in place. That long-term plan is the working of the Holy Spirit in our daily Christian lives.

Yes, it is God's will that the redeemed are eternally guided by his Spirit of truth. God loves each one us—the redeemed in his Son—so much that he has set his Holy Spirit within our saved souls. This one truth standing on its own should bring great joy into your Christian life. I pray your life in the Holy Spirit will be one of immense fulfilment—so much so that you will yearn to understand his daily importance in all our lives, and this in cooperation with the redeemed of Jesus, as we celebrate life on Earth and eternal life beyond.

Does God have a plan for you? Yes, he does! He has lovingly placed within your redeemed soul the active daily guidance of the Holy Spirit! Begin a personal relationship with the Holy Spirit today, and be awakened to your life in Christ Jesus—the one who promised *you* his Holy Spirit. Meet the promise Jesus faithfully ushered into your life when you accepted him as Lord and Savior.

Yes! It all began with love!

Part 1

CHAPTER 1

Off to a Good Start?

As we begin the first steps of our journey, I'd like to personally say to you that I am truly grateful first to God and his Holy Spirit–inspired Word, the Bible, for the instruction and learning I've received over the years. The Holy Spirit became a subject of interest to me when I realized that Jesus sent him to us for a purpose. This purpose can be missed if we allow all the nuts and bolts of theology or a lack of understanding to override the subject himself–namely the Holy Spirit.

Through all the books God placed in my hands—each accompanied by the Bible—I excitedly began writing about the Holy Spirit. Hundreds of pages poured forth. Though undoubtedly the focus was centered on the Holy Spirit, what was truly on my heart I had difficulty conveying in a practical, everyday way. I tried numerous approaches, and I had many exciting beginnings that took off with great exuberance. It seemed I could get my thoughts running, but I continually felt there was a missing link from my standpoint—one that the Lord openly revealed to me during a time of unexpected illness. After six weeks of downtime, I was refreshed, and the missing link of my original thoughts had unveiled itself.

As untimely as my sudden illness seemed, God used the event to help me get dialed in. He uses circumstances to tune us in to his great wisdom and will. The Holy Spirit was most assuredly at work, and I was going to be led to the front door of God's purpose; the Spirit residing in my saved soul would soon jump off the page and, with indisputable evidence, become to me *the* person I was in hopes of writing about.

Everything was well on the morning of April 27, 2016. My wife and I were up and about. Breakfast—a healthy bowl of cereal—was satisfying. My routine of enjoying retirement and initiating the no-rush plan for the day was put into gear. Doing some touch-up painting on the patio was in order, as I planned to hang a few new ceiling fans before the summer heat soon arrived.

As I was reaching over my head to apply the finishing stroke of paint, I Immediately felt a sharp, excruciating pain in my right shoulder blade. I decided I'd pulled a muscle and should quit for the day; this was not my norm. Though the pain was intense, I made sure to meticulously seal the paint can, as is my nature. After making my way into the laundry room to clean my brush, just as I began the process, I felt a searing pain clenching the center of my chest. I shut off the water and told Elaine I wasn't feeling well and needed to go to the living room to sit in my recliner. As I ambled into the room and sat down, the pain intensified—massively intensified. Elaine, concerned, said she would call the doctor. I told her we needed to say our good-byes because I wasn't going to make it. By that time, I felt as though I were stuck in a place from where I could not get out. The pain of death—the killing pain—was clenching me with its unrelenting gripped fist. I knew then I was having a heart attack, though I had never experienced such a terrible pain in my life.

As I was feverishly grasping my dear wife's hand, I saw a group of papers I had been proofing the night before. They were a portion of my manuscript of the book I was writing on the Holy Spirit. In my desperation, I asked Elaine, by way of direction, to make sure to get the work to my friend Shane. I felt confident he could put the finishing touches on the text so it could be published. Despite my last-minute request, I remember thinking, *all those words on paper aren't really what I think they should be.* They weren't going to be any different from the other books I had read on the Holy Spirit. They were a repetition at best.

Elaine gave no response to my appeal. The only thing she centered her attention on was getting me into our truck and rushing me to the hospital, which was ten minutes away. She did just that.

God had other plans for me as far as the writing of this book. He was going to use my downtime—unbeknown to me—to open my eyes to the Holy Spirit as seen from a different light. He was going to reveal to me, in my heart, the love that began it all.

This insight would prove to be an eye-opener for me, since it was the approach I seemed to have relentlessly looked for but could not seem to bring into view. It would take a traumatic time to reveal the actual working of the person of God—the Holy Spirit—I was attempting to communicate to my Christian brothers and sisters. Through this time of turmoil, the Lord reached into my soul and pulled back the curtain I had erected from childhood—a lingering subconscious barrier of being frightened of the Holy Ghost.

Though I felt the early onset of fear was long behind me by the time I really noticed the Holy Spirit in my life, there was obviously a lack of true acceptance. He was, after many years, still a bit of a stranger to me. And while the research I had done was bringing awareness, it was doing so only in the sense of head knowledge and not of heart experience.

I spent many hours writing of personal experiences, especially focusing on my childhood, to somewhat justify the peace I felt I had at that time from the presence of the Lord's Spirit. By way of another approach, I set out to write a handbook designed to be a quick reference for the Christian to bring about daily awareness of the Spirit.

9

On and on I plugged away, trying to manufacture a book that would say or simplify things no other books had. Another avenue I went down produced several hundred pages of what-if scenarios assembled with the thinking that they would provoke the soul while being a useful tool for awareness and need—one where the Holy Spirit would become very evident in the Christian reader's life. With all not being lost, I believe the Holy Spirit himself has used each of these approaches to set the stage for me to freely write from my heart while depending upon the Word of God as the true center line.

I had lots of time to soul-search and pray during the heart attack experience and on into the results of the surgery and the recovery. My Bible became a daily tool of insight. The Lord led me to places throughout the entire book that I had not really searched out before. One place he took me was to the beginning. It was there he confirmed in my heart his reason for creating you and me. An illuminating confirmation of this truth was confirmed through an exhortation Jesus made thousands of years later.

What an eye-opening experience this afforded for me as a basis of why God has placed his Holy Spirit in our souls and in the soul of each saved one of Jesus Christ.

What was the grand ingredient of God's plan for you and me?

CHAPTER 2

From a Different Perspective

It all began with love. **Yes!**

That's the revelation God laid on my heart. It's a truth I've been aware of for years. My mother's love made it very well known that Jesus loved me very much too. She forgave me for hiding something from her and from my dad—a two-dollar pocket watch they lovingly gave me for my birthday. One time I even dunked it in my friend's aquarium just to see if it was waterproof, dangling the treasured timekeeper from the end of its gold-colored chain amid the tropical fish. Unfortunately, the water-filled plastic crystal and blurred black-ink numbers revealed the ugly fact to a frightened and broken eight-year-old heart: the once ticking watch was no longer a prized timepiece; it was an object of shame that was sure to bring punishment or even abandonment. The only thing to do was to hide the defunct mess in my underwear drawer—a smart thing for a kid to do, but not so brilliant when it came to the fact that my grandmother discovered it through her routine washing.

When lovingly summoned by Mom into my bedroom—one my older brother and I shared equally—I was asked to produce the birthday watch. Reluctantly, I opened the drawer of choice, nervously grabbed it, and laid it on my mom's open right hand. Mama looked up at me as she was sitting on my bed. I was heartbroken. My only focus at that point was the tears flowing down her cheeks. They were real tears!

That day I felt as if the world had come to an end. I had never seen my mom cry over something because of my own doing. I was devastated, and my heart was aching. Mama told me that I had hurt her and my dad by what I'd done. After a good cry shared between us, Mama said to me, "I forgive you, and so does Jesus." I told my mom in my serious eight-year-old tone that I couldn't face Jesus because I had hurt her and Daddy and Jesus too. With a loving embrace, Mama told me that Jesus would never disown me as I had feared. She said, "Jesus is love, and he loves you too much to let you go." She impressed upon me that what I had done was wrong, but that it was a mistake even though I willfully acted on my own.

For a brokenhearted boy, it all began with love. Even from a moment of indiscretion, the love of God was revealed—a lasting love that will endure and never end. Yes! Jesus was the center of my life even when I was as young as eight. Unbeknown to me, the Holy Spirit was his gift living within my saved soul. It would take many years for me to allow him his place within, as Jesus was whom I considered my best friend.

Over the span of my Christian life, I didn't consider the importance of the Holy Spirit. I knew he existed, but I was ignorant to the truth of his residing within my soul. Even in times of knowing the Lord's moving in my life, I always considered the tangible Jesus to be the one doing the moving. A good portion of the problem came because of my lack of Bible exposure. It wasn't until I was in my forties that God introduced me to the Bible in a serious way. I took it in as if I were a sponge. I was made aware of the Holy Spirit through the Gospels and Letters, but I still clung to Jesus.

There came a time when the Lord revealed the Holy Spirit to me with great impact. It happened by way of a study I was doing in John 14. The revelation popped off the page and opened the reality to me that Jesus, when he made his promise to the disciples the night he was arrested, would send *himself* back to them as the Counselor—the Spirit of truth. That's where the first bell rang in my heart. Though I still had a hard time letting Jesus do his work in my heart by way of his Holy Spirit, eventually I surrendered—and what joy he allowed me to have as a Christian! It is truth that God is present everywhere. I'll be the first to agree. The bottom line is that Jesus is physically in heaven with the Father, and his Holy Spirit is right here in you and me and every redeemed soul. That one revelation swung open the door that set me on a journey of desire to share the Holy Spirit and his vital importance in your daily Christian life and beyond.

As a pastor, I have preached several thousand sermons and have taught hundreds of classes on the Lord. I have emphasized God's love, as well as the idea that God *is* love. As much as I've studied the Bible and discussed it with family and my congregations, I have not for one second denied God's love for each one of us as Christians. It is out of the evident love of the Lord Jesus Christ—God's one and only Son—who unselfishly died on the cross for the forgiveness of our sins, that we are secure in his love. This is love the world cannot give, as hard as it may try. Agape love (pronounced ah-gah-pay) is love that *is* God himself. He is the absolute Source of this ultimate bestowal. He is the outpouring of the only true love man, woman, and child will ever know as genuine.

This is the eureka moment God gave me over the past six weeks of rereading several of my books on the Holy Spirit. No matter how complex the study or how simple the explanation given, all are confirmed by the book of books—the Bible. The crowning glory of the review has come by way of the Bible itself. Through the research and study, I've been blessed to do over the years, there has come a different light by way of realizing this one truth—the truth that before any existence as we know it, *God was love,* and that everything began as a result of this absolute love. For me this truth is more than confirmed. It began with my attachment to Jesus and has wonderfully unfolded through the Holy Spirit. Now that I've had years of opportunity to learn about the Holy Spirit from Genesis to Revelation, it is my honor to share with you the evident truth that began it all—*love.* **Yes!** It all began with love.

When God was creating the world, the Bible tells us in Genesis 1:2 that the Spirit of God was hovering over the waters. Imagine, if you will, a mother hen. During times of uncertainty, such when there is a perceived threat to her chicks, she holds her wings open and calls to her brood to come to her for safety. It is the hovering of this loving mother that gives security to the little ones. In a similar way, we can imagine that God—namely his Spirit—was hovering over his creation as it was taking shape. It is this attentive love that has no beginning or end that he was exercising and genuinely demonstrating to all that was to follow. This excitedly includes you and me. His unblemished genuine agape love is that which is exercised and demonstrated by the same Spirit that hovered over the waters in the beginning.

Take a moment to ponder this reality. The Spirit of God, out of ultimate love, hovered over creation as it was happening and is right now living within you as your Guide, Counselor, and Sustainer. God, the source of absolute love, set his Spirit in the heavens to hover over an incomplete world and now is set within your completed redeemed soul through the sacrificial love of Jesus. How wonderful is this that we should give full attention to the Holy Spirit daily! Do you want this gift to be continually exercised within you and completely recognized by you? God surely does! Read on.

CHAPTER 3

Confirmed Authenticated Agape

From the confirmed Source of love—that which existed from no beginning—moving forward as if through the sands of time, take note of the confirmation of this continual agape as authenticated by Jesus Christ the Son. Through these few words of genuine truth, hear what Jesus says to the Father in perfect witness: "and I will continue to make you known in order that the love you have for me may be in them and that I myself may be in them" (John 17:26).

Hear additionally what Jesus witnessed to the Father just a few beautiful words prior to the former. "Father, I want those you have given me to be with me where I am, and to see my glory, the glory you have given me because *you loved me* before the creation of the world" (John 17: 24, emphasis added).

"*You loved me* before the creation of the world." These words are confirming authentication spoken to the Father by his Son and are proof positive that before the first iota of creation took place, the love of God was in full force. His agape love was the identification of his absolute being, who has existed from no beginning and carries through the ages with no end. Could there be any clearer confirmation than that of the true witness between the voice of Jesus—God the Son—and the hearing of God the Father, and as acted out in the continual working of the Holy Spirit—the Spirit of God—today, just as he has been actively functioning since eternity past?

Without a doubt, the love of God abounds eternally. Christian, it is this agape love that has saved your very soul as a redeemed one of the Lord Jesus Christ. This almost undefinable heart of love is the same agape that eternally embraced Jesus the Son before the world was brought into existence. It is the same as that demonstrated by the Holy Spirit at the beginning of creation. This is the hinge of the fruitful future intended for you and every believer saved by the shed blood of Jesus Christ. The culmination of the Father, Son, and Holy Spirit is very evident as Jesus testifies of the working agape love evident then and now.

It is because of the eternal, unchanging love of the Father for you and me and whosoever will believe that Jesus Christ suffered on the cross. Out of this endless permeating possession within his divine soul—that which was of the Father from eternity past—Jesus made full payment for our sin. The ugly nemesis, sin, that separated mankind, God's creation, from God was wiped out by the precious blood of Jesus—the eternally loved Son of God.

This eternal affection had to be made manifest—evident—in the saved souls of the redeemed. Jesus knew this and acted on it by conveying the Father's agape first to the disciples and then to us. Hear what Jesus promised the disciples the night he was arrested.

Gathered around the table with eleven of the disciples (having earlier sent Judas Iscariot to do his deed of betraying him into the hands of his accusers as was prophesied), Jesus was fully aware he must make a lasting promise. It was one of divine conveyance he would initially put in motion in the minds and hearts of the eleven. This divine promise would be of eternal endurance for them, and it would also, importantly and universally, woven with the golden cord of agape love, carry forward for each redeemed believer for ages into the future.

Jesus said,

> If you love me, you will obey what I command. And I will
> ask the Father, and he will give you *another Counselor to
> be with you forever—the Spirit of truth*. The world cannot
> accept him, because it neither sees him nor knows him.
> But you know him, for he lives with you *and will be in
> you*. I will not leave you as orphans; *I will come to you*.
> Before long, the world will not see me. Because I live,
> you also will live. On that day *you will realize* that I am in
> my Father, and you are in me, *and I am in you*. (John 14:
> 15—20, emphasis added)

So many times, early on, I read this promise of promises. There
is no doubt I understood it, to a point. Jesus promised this to the
disciples and has carried it on to affect me and every believer. The
Spirit of truth—the Counselor—was truly involved with progressively
sanctifying the saved. In my early days, I missed the point of the
Holy Spirit's daily association with me. As I understood it, the Holy
Spirit, no doubt, had a significant job to do. I was fine with that.
Because I had placed my entire life in the hands of Jesus, as I earlier
mentioned, it was difficult for me to let the Holy Spirit in so he
could carry on the work assigned him as part of God's divine plan.
He was, in fact, fulfilling his end of the plan, but I was blind to his
intended personal relationship with me. His guiding eventually did
open me to his love, which was the very same as that of the Father
and the Son. Once the Spirit revealed himself to me through the
above scripture, I completely surrendered to his guiding. I gave the
Holy Spirit the place God assigned in my saved soul. Jesus had come
through. His initial promise to the disciples, and consecutively to you
and me and every redeemed believer, was opened to me as realized
truth. This truth absolutely set me free. My heart was excited, and I
wanted to know more of the Royal Resident—the Spirit of the Lord.

The entirety of John 14:15—21 came alive right before my eyes.
Though I had reluctantly determined to know him, I wasn't completely

allowing the door open to his eternal authority as ushered in by the Father and the Son. Thanks to the Holy Spirit's guiding and counsel, the needed change has come. Confirmed authentication—agape love—has set my spirit free in him, and he is ready and willing to do the same for you.

I pray what you have read so far has set the stage for the rest of this writing. You, the redeemed believer, have the promise living within your soul. He is the embodiment of the Father and the Son. He *is* the Holy Spirit—the Spirit of truth. It is out of an unchangeable love that you are indwelled eternally. This never-ending agape love existing from no beginning, the Spirit of God, undeniably and willingly occupies your saved soul. From Jesus's testimony, are you now aware of the reason God has placed himself within you? It's God's divine purpose, and the beginning of the purpose is *love!*

Allow the Holy Spirit to guide you into all truth as you continue the journey. Let's enjoy this exciting journey together.

CHAPTER 4

Of Daily Importance

From what you've learned so far, has the Holy Spirit taken on a new meaning in your life as a Christian? How would you convey your thought to another Christian? How do you see the Holy Spirit as being an integral part of your Christian life?

God desires the Holy Spirit to permanently reside in your redeemed soul. If it were not out of his complete love for you, God would not be a part of you. He could have taken it as a great insult when the first man and woman disobeyed his command and willfully followed the lead of the evil one. Because of such a possible insult, God could have abandoned the whole project, and you and I and all of creation would be moot. Thank God! He was not insulted to the point of pulling the plug. It was already in his wisdom and knowledge that man could falter. The reason for this is that God gave man a free will. That free will continues as a part of each person born into this world. And you still have a free will to allow the Holy Spirit to be of utmost importance in your saved condition or to mundanely amble through Christianity, making yourself vulnerable to the world's sway. Whatever your current condition, God still loves you beyond measure. Nonetheless, his Spirit—the Holy Spirit—resides within your redeemed soul and is ready and willing to work through you as you allow him to do so. Are you compelled to let the Holy Spirit work through you?

Where do you want to be? I can tell you where God wants you to be. Listen to the words of Jesus Christ before he went to the cruel cross of Calvary. "For God so loved the world, that He gave His only begotten Son, that whosoever believeth in Him should not perish, but have everlasting life. For God sent not His Son into the world to condemn the world; but that the world through Him might be saved" (John 3:16–17 KJV).

Christian, you are saved! You are one of the "whosoever." You believe in the sacrifice of Jesus on the cross for the forgiveness of your once sin-darkened soul. You were reunited with God the Father! It is the love Jesus iterates within this verse of Holy Scripture that expresses to the utmost God's agape love for you before you were saved; and now you *are* saved and redeemed by the perfect blood of the Son, Jesus. How important is this fact of love to you? If God loved you so much before you were reunited with him through Jesus and the indwelling Holy Spirit, how much more do you feel the Father loves you and desires you to be completely open to him now?

Take a moment. Recap your stance in Jesus since you received him as Lord and Savior. What awareness did you have of the Holy Spirit at that magnificent moment? To what degree was his presence acknowledged by you? Since that wonderful day, have you spoken to him or asked for blessing and advice daily?

You now know you have the gift freely given you by the Father through the work of Jesus on the cross. Do you feel uplifted? It is vital you acknowledge the truth always. Just as he is in permanent residence in your soul, the Spirit of God is completely present to guide, counsel, and progressively sanctify you as his own. Begin to understand his truth, beginning with love, and your relationship with him will blossom and bloom each day of your Christian life. It is of great importance that you daily share your life with the Holy Spirit. It is equally as important that you allow him to guide you with his Word.

His Word—Your Heart

Do you have a Bible in your possession? If not, please acquire one as soon as possible. Let me point you to what God's Word says about God's word. "For the word of God is living and active. Sharper than any double-edged sword, it penetrates even to dividing soul and spirit, joints and marrow; it judges the thoughts and attitudes of the heart" (Hebrews 4:12).

Do you know why the Word of God is so powerful and alive? It is of great importance to you that God's Word be in front of you daily and that his Spirit be actively working through you. Because God's Word is in your hands and heart, the Holy Spirit is powerfully guiding, counseling, and sanctifying you. He is the Inspirer and Author of the divine Word. Listen to him speak this to you through the apostle Paul: "All Scripture is God-breathed and is useful for teaching, rebuking, correcting and training in righteousness, so that the man of God may be thoroughly equipped for every good work" (2 Timothy 3:16).

Combining the two passages of scripture—God's living, active, God-breathed Word—it is plain to see there is power beyond measure at your fingertips, if you will daily allow him to speak to you through his Word. If the Holy Spirit inspired the Word and he lives within your redeemed soul, it is out of God's immense *love* for you that he desires for you to know him, listen to him, and ask for his daily guidance. It is through the Holy Spirit that the Father's agape love works through you as his representative of the Lord Jesus each day of your life.

Through reading God's Word daily, the Holy Spirit will instruct you on living a quality, exciting Christian life. The Gospels are a wonderful lesson of godly living as we are instructed by Jesus's perfect life. We are, by the guiding of the Holy Spirit, which Jesus promised and delivered to us, inspired and enlightened in the way Jesus expects us to live as his ambassadors. We represent his goodness, graciousness, and godliness. And all this is enveloped in the greatest love ever—agape love.

By representing Christ Jesus through this powerful love, we set the desired example for him to the world around us and to our brothers and sisters in Christ. It is this power possessed within—being indwelled and filled with the Holy Spirit—that is of daily importance to you, me, and every other Christian. A constant awareness of the Holy Spirit is of such importance that you can't afford to be lax for one moment. As part of Jesus's prayer, he first taught the disciples to pray, "and lead us not into temptation, but deliver us from the evil one." It is pertinent you and I are prepared for the onslaught of the world. We are surely in it, but we are **not** of it.

The Holy Spirit is willing and ready 24-7 to lead and guide you into all truth through the Word of God. Open your Bible today and hear the Word of truth as you allow your redeemed soul to be strengthened. This is of daily importance to you. Welcome the Holy Spirit to be your forever Guide.

Are you getting excited about your Eternal Resident? I hope you are. The more I write, the more excited I am to know we are in this together and we have the greatest love and power within us—the Holy Spirit.

CHAPTER 5

Awareness through Roadblocks

How many roadblocks can you recall that have potentially been nemeses in your Christian life: A bad day at the workplace? A negative beginning to your day by way of an argument with your spouse or maybe your child? How about something major, such as the loss of a precious friend due to the senseless act of an inattentive motorist? These are just a few ideas that could suggest roadblocks put in the path of your Christian walk.

Early on I mentioned recently having had a severe heart attack. As it was occurring, I felt I was going to step into eternity to be with my Lord. If this had happened, obviously, I would not be penning these thoughts to you. Though I was not taken home by the Lord, I felt as if I had directly stumbled upon an almost immovable roadblock. One reason for this was that I had a precious wife I was concerned about regarding how she was going to maintain the daily responsibilities of our home and property. Another concern was that I felt I had failed by not having completed the book I had been writing for several years. Our children came to mind. There was one son I needed to come to peace with over a misunderstanding that had separated us for several years. I needed to resolve the issue whether he wanted to or not. It's amazing how many things can scuttle through the mind when such an intense moment is in the works.

At this point, before I get into roadblocks and how to cope with them, it is very important that you come to a complete understanding of you being a Christian.

You, Christian, are redeemed by the precious blood of Jesus Christ that spilled from his body as he anguished in intense torment and pain while cruelly hanging from the cross of Calvary. This act of complete unselfishness was carried out by Jesus for you through complete obedience to the Father that your sin would be forgiven, making way for you to be reunited with the Father. He lovingly gave his perfect life for you by shouldering your sin and the sin of the entire world—past, present, and future—to bridge the gap that once separated you from the Father. It was Jesus, "the only begotten Son of God" who could singly carry out this act of agape love. And just imagine—he did it for you!

Jesus's love was not completely encompassed at Calvary. His act of complete love accompanied him to the grave and beyond. On the third day, as Jesus had promised and as had been earlier prophesied, Jesus rose from the dead by the power of God. So, you could share with him eternal life, he was obedient. By way of Jesus carrying out the command of the Father, you and "whosoever will believe" are completely secure in this truth.

With forgiveness of your sins being firmly in place, the absolute love of God dwells within your redeemed soul. The Holy Spirit is your permanent resident. At this very moment, he is eternally living within your saved soul. The Holy Spirit is whom Jesus promised to you and me through his first disciples. Remember? Jesus, on the night he was to be arrested, promised the disciples that he would send himself back—by way of the Spirit of truth, the Holy Spirit—and that he would indwell each redeemed believer. This magnificent truth, though the disciples didn't quite grasp it now, did, in fact, come to fruition.

The Holy Spirit, by way of Jesus's ultimate unconditional sacrifice, was delivered by the Father at the specified initial time and would be continually carried out upon the salvation of each believing man, woman, and child. The introductory coming of the Holy Spirit into the saved soul of each redeemed believer occurred on the Day of Pentecost. This was the initiation of the universal powerful working of the Holy Spirit for those who received him that wonderful day, as well as for you and me and all who do believe and will believe in the future. More will be explained during the unfolding of the pages before you.

The stage has been set. You basically understand your God-ordained position as a Christian loved by the Father, Son, and Holy Spirit. It is important that you grasp this vital truth. It is through this you will begin to know in your heart how the Holy Spirit is working nonstop in your Christian life. Here is a wonderful continuance for you to become more acquainted with the Spirit of truth given to you out of the agape love of the Father, through the ultimate sacrifice of Jesus and the joyful action of the Holy Spirit entering and now residing within your cleansed soul. This ultimate truth standing before you and me will be of great help. It will shed divine light to help assist in better understanding the idea of facing roadblocks during our Christian walk and in the many aspects of living life in this everyday world. Roadblocks spring up in our Christian lives unannounced and without hesitation.

I had no Idea a heart attack would jump up before me that unsuspecting day. The bottom line is that it did, and I had to deal with the circumstances. Had I not believed, by way of God's Word, that I truly had residing within my soul the Spirit of Jesus, whom I love dearly, I can't imagine what kind of thoughts would have been occupying my mind.

It was the *love* of God I failed to give more attentive thought to, in relation to his embracing my soul during such an event—one where I could have squarely fallen short and could also have easily succumbed to panic.

Though I may not have been completely focused on the reason he was guiding me to help you understand a shortcoming I was guilty of, I can tell you I was aware the Holy Spirit was there. It was through such a shocking moment and during the following days and weeks—even today as I continue to recover with a repaired heart—that I came to realize more affirmatively the presence of the agape love of God within my soul. He is here to stay and will always guide us through all circumstances, and this is possible through his immense eternal agape love for each of us. This is such a wide-open truth to be missed by distraction. This doesn't need to be. Continual awareness is key.

Roadblocks may seem to be difficult to handle, but the Spirit living within our redeemed souls has the resolve each time. Here is where you may have a disagreeing thought. You may be thinking that what I am iterating to you is ideal. You may also be thinking life is far from ideal. Let assurance come into your heart and mind by way of the truth—the ideal truth that never falters. Jesus tells us—we Christians—he will never leave us or forsake us. He also tells us that we are not to be afraid; Jesus's continuing promise to you and me and every redeemed Christian is that he has given us his peace, and this peace is a living part of his Holy Spirit, who entered our souls the moment we accepted him as Lord and Savior. Jesus's promise is ideal and eternal. His promises are completely binding, and the witness of these promises is held out before us as final truth by the Father, Son, and Holy Spirit. Let not the swaying of the world mess with your mind or heart. Take it as absolute truth; what God says stands forever. Allow the Holy Spirit to truly reside within your redeemed soul, out of the agape love of the Father and his Son, to be alive within you as you give him his place in your Christian life to walk with you every inch of the way. Let the Holy Spirit be your eternal Guide as he walks you through the trying circumstances of the minor and major roadblocks of life. We are reminded by the apostle Paul through the guiding of the Holy Spirit that we can do all things through him who strengthens us—namely the Spirit of Jesus living through absolute love within us (that love being the agape love that loved Jesus before the creation and that flows as a stream of living water within our souls and continues to flow from our souls into the world around us). This is *his* love.

There was not one roadblock Jesus faced that he was not able to overcome. And it was through his faithfulness and strength that he promised us the Holy Spirit, whom we now have as our Guide, Counselor, and Sustainer. It is through the power of the Holy Spirit that we are given strength to face the roadblocks.

CHAPTER 6

Speaking of Streams

During my recovery time, I've had the opportunity to review truths concerning benchmarks of the Holy Spirit. One of these markers is found in the prophecy of Ezekiel, and many generations later it was fulfilled by Jesus in Jerusalem. It involves a river of water and streams of water.

Flowing water has a character about it. Its movement can be subtle, rushing, or somewhere in between. The river and the streams can be teeming with life or desolate; they can be placid or tumultuous. Depending upon the geography and the circumstances, the waters display their character.

In comparison between the prophecy of Ezekiel and the fulfilment of it by Jesus—and the continued fulfilment as found in the Revelation of Jesus Christ—I would further like to share the agape love the Father has for you, his redeemed.

Let's look at the promise Jesus made in Jerusalem as he stood in the temple courts. "On the last and greatest day of the Feast, Jesus stood and said in a loud voice, 'If anyone is thirsty, let him come to me and drink. Whoever believes in me, as the Scripture has said, streams of living water will flow from within him.' By this he meant the Spirit, whom those who believed in him were later to receive. Up to that time the Spirit had not yet been given, since Jesus had not yet been glorified'" (John 7:37–39).

This scripture is very important, with Jesus's final days on Earth in view while the first segment of his mission was coming to completion. He would soon be going to the cross. Jesus was speaking of the "streams of living water," pointing to himself, who was to come back as the Holy Spirit. He called out to "whosoever" and carried the calling with his promise to the disciples as well as to us, as is found in John 14:16.

Now let's travel back in time to the prophecy of Ezekiel concerning the river of water.

> The man brought me back to the entrance of the temple, and I saw water coming out from under the threshold of the temple toward the east (for the temple faced east). The water was coming down from under the south side of the temple, south of the altar. He then brought me out through the north gate and led me around the outside to the outer gate facing east, and the water was flowing from the south side.

> As the man went eastward with a measuring line in his hand, he measured off a thousand cubits and then led me through water that was ankle-deep. He measured off another thousand cubits and led me through water that was knee-deep. He measured off another thousand and led me through water that was up to the waste. He measured off another thousand, but now it was a river that I could not cross, because the water had risen and was deep enough to swim in—a river that no one could cross. He asked me, "Son of man, do you see this?"

> Then he led me back to the bank of the river. When I arrived there, I saw a great number of trees on each

side of the river. He said to me, "This water flows from the eastern region and goes down into Arabah, where it enters the Sea. When it empties into the Sea, the water there becomes fresh. Swarms of living creatures will live wherever the river flows. There will be large numbers of fish, because this water flows there and makes the salt water fresh; so, where the river flows everything will live. Fishermen will stand along the shore; from En Gedi to En Eglaim there will be places for spreading nets. The fish will be of many kinds—like the fish of the Great Sea. But the swamps and marshes will not become fresh; they will be left for salt. Fruit trees of all kinds will grow on both banks of the river. Their leaves will not wither, nor will their fruit fail. Every month they will bear, because the water from the sanctuary flows to them. Their fruit will serve for food and their leaves for healing." (Ezekiel 47:1–12)

This passage out of Ezekiel may sound a bit complex (which it theologically can be), but in respect to what Jesus said in a loud voice from the temple courts and later in Revelation, I believe you will become excited and embrace the importance of the Holy Spirit in your life as a Christian.

The last day of the feast in Jerusalem was one of great importance. Per Leviticus, "The Lord said to Moses, 'Say to the Israelites: "On the fifteenth day of the seventh month the Lord's Feast of Tabernacles begins, and it lasts for seven days. The first day is a sacred assembly; do no regular work. For seven days, present offerings made to the Lord by fire, and on the eighth day hold a sacred assembly and present an offering made to the Lord by fire. It is the closing assembly; do no regular work"'" (Leviticus 23: 33–36).

When Jesus spoke out loud as he was in the temple courts, it was the last and greatest day of the feast (the Feast of Tabernacles). This day had wonderful significance. It was a day of demarcation.

It was the day when the Lord Jesus announced the Holy Spirit. Though the people did not understand now what Jesus was doing, they did hear his words of invitation. He was marking the end of his physical ministry here on earth, as it was soon to end. He was calling to mind the prophecy of Ezekiel concerning the streams of water and the river. He was announcing himself as the "streams of living water" that would flow from within them, and this would be true of whoever believed in him. His beginning words say in such a love-filled way, "If anyone is thirsty, let him come and drink."

Bringing the experience Ezekiel recorded into view is the action Jesus brings to life. The original water Ezekiel saw flowing from under the threshold of the temple was only the beginning of the precious water of life expressed by Jesus as an open invitation to the believer. You, Christian, are a believer, and this living water has been springing up through you since the day you received Jesus into your life. The river teeming with life is living within your redeemed soul!

Looking at the prophecy from a geographical standpoint tells us that the river flows into the "Sea" at "Arabah." Arabah is at the Salt Sea—the Dead Sea, which so happens to be the lowest land point on earth. Water from the Jordan River flows into this mass of salt-saturated water just to become lifeless because of the end of flow. The water flowing into it literally has nowhere else to flow. It turns into a highly-concentrated saltwater mass. Lifelessness is the norm.

Per Ezekiel, the water flowing from the temple into the "Sea" (represented by the Dead Sea) made a massive change in the region. Saltwater was turned into life-filled, fresh, freely flowing water. Great fruit-bearing trees were evident and bore wonderful fruit, and the leaves of the trees were good for healing.

I mentioned Revelation relating to the Ezekiel prophecy. This is the end-times prophecy in which John was instructed to record all he saw. "Then the angel showed me the river of the water of life, as clear as crystal, flowing from the throne of God and the Lamb down the middle of the great street of the city. On each side of the river stood the tree of life, bearing twelve crops of fruit every month. And the leaves of the tree are for the healing of the nations" (Revelation 22: 1–2).

Now that you have had a taste of the prophecy of Ezekiel concerning the flowing water and the river, and the action of invitation Jesus gave on the last and greatest day of the feast, I have exciting news for you. Read on and discover how personal the Holy Spirit is to you.

CHAPTER 7

What Is Your Depth

The first thing Ezekiel saw was the water flowing out from under the threshold of the temple. By the way, the temple is God's sanctuary. In the days of Ezekiel, and even the days of Jesus, the temple was God's earthly house. In the early days of the temple, the one built by the hands of man, the ark of the covenant—the Presence of God—was housed in the most sacred room, known as the Holy of Holies. In Jesus's day, the temple had been reconstructed. The Presence of God was still there, as we learn in the gospel of Luke that the future father of John the Baptist, Zechariah, was a priest of the division of Abijah and was in service at the temple. "Once when Zechariah's division was on duty and he was serving as priest before God, he was chosen by lot, to go into the temple of the Lord to burn incense. And when the time for the burning of incense came, all the assembled worshipers were praying outside" (Luke 1:8–10). This was about a year or so before Jesus was born.

After Jesus's triumphal entry into Jerusalem—the week before he went to the cross—where he would partake in the Passover for the last time, Jesus entered the temple and was less than happy with what he found. "Then he entered the temple area and began driving out those who were selling. 'It is written,' he said to them, '"My house will be a house of prayer"; but you have made it "a den of robbers"'" (Luke 19:45–46). God's sacred temple was being defiled by profiteers. This earthly temple was prescribed by God and was to remain holy, as was the temple Ezekiel saw. God's presence is to be ultimately respected and revered as his sanctuary no matter whether it is in the desert wilderness or in Jerusalem or the New Jerusalem.

With the sacred scene of the prophecy of Ezekiel in place, Jesus confirmed the flowing water— "streams of living water"—as the sacredness of God the Holy Spirit. He was publicly inviting anyone who would believe to come and drink. This invitation of Jesus on that last and greatest day of the feast rings out through eternity. The Holy Spirit, now in place, beckons all who will believe to receive the forgiveness of Jesus and his free gift of salvation and eternal life.

As I was reviewing the prophecy of Ezekiel and savoring the beautiful scene, I was brought to a place where I visualized the stream of water flowing from under the threshold of the temple—God's sacred dwelling place—and I watched Ezekiel and the man with the measuring line. As the man led Ezekiel the first thousand cubits, I sensed the ankle-deep water, which seemed so refreshing. The next thousand-cubit length leading into knee-deep refreshment was more inviting. After a moment of being in the knee-deep environment, I sensed the desire to go further. Waist-deep was more satisfying, but only for a moment was I content. I was excited to go the rest of the distance of the river. I was moved to go headlong into the river of life! This is a place I had never visited as a Christian. My spirit was given fresh awareness.

After spiritually plunging into the beauty, I asked myself, as if I were asking my congregation, "How deep do you want to go? What is your depth? Are you satisfied with your present place with the Holy Spirit? Are you okay with being ankle deep, or do you desire to be completely covered, fully submerged in the river of life—the Holy Spirit?" From that point, I knew the answer.

Revisiting the heart attack experience, I admit I've had a lot of time to soul-search. Though I have read the Bible daily for many years and have received blessing upon blessing, the Holy Spirit has used the past six weeks, and counting, to set my spirit straight with him and to give me the opportunity to understand the depth of his love for me—the love I've been sharing with you since the beginning of this book.

What is your depth? What is your depth with the Holy Spirit now that you have been exposed to the previous chapters contained within the Word of God, active and alive—the truth only the Holy Spirit can lead you into? He loves you and wants you to be fully submerged in him. Are you willing to be there?

As I continue to write to you, I am excited! The love of God is completely immersing me in his truth. The will of the Father, Jesus has iterated, is coming more and more alive. The sacrifice of Jesus is always engulfing my spirit. The Holy Spirit has a more prominent place in my life than I ever realized. *Yes! It All Began with Love* has such meaning to me that I will share it with the world, because I now know the Lord has broken through that I should share not his complexity but his practicality in my life and the potentiality of the same in your life. He is a God of unfathomable love. He is a God of unconditional sacrifice and *the* God of extreme presence!

Let's continue our journey together with the Holy Spirit as he guides us into all truth. What's your depth? Are you truly alive in spirit?

Lifelessness Made Alive

In thinking about the depth of our spirit in relation to the invitation of the Holy Spirit, there is another view to consider. The prophecy of Ezekiel not only showed a beautiful picture of the progressive depth of the water that originated from the temple, but also recalled its destination. Ultimately it flowed to the barren region known as the "Sea." As I mentioned, the "Sea" is the Dead Sea, which is the lowest land point on earth. The unfortunate thing is that it has no outlet. Whatever flows into it remains and becomes useless to life.

Lifelessness is the sad state there. The water that flows into this "Sea" today continues to become lifeless as the magnitude of salt concentration takes the life right out of that which flows into it.

On the other hand, consider the good news of the prophecy of Ezekiel. The water flowing from the temple—which became a river of depth and great width, active with life—flowed into the "Sea," which was a barren mass of nonproductive highly concentrated saltwater incapable of supporting life.

By the miracle of God, and out of his absolute love, there came a revelation to Ezekiel. This unveiling pointed toward the future from the prophet's day and was directed toward a future truth as being related to what will occur at the coming of the New Jerusalem, when Jesus consummates his kingdom. This prophecy not only pointed toward the eternal Jerusalem; it also related to the soul of lost man. It pointed toward your soul and mine. Because God is personal to each of his created ones, he has given each man, woman, and child the choice to either accept or reject his loving, life-filled provision.

With the stage of the flowing river of life set, picture this eternal river as flowing from God into your soul, which was once as barren as the Dead Sea. You were lost up to the moment you asked Jesus's forgiveness for your sin and invited him into your once barren soul. The darkness of sin covered it. Had you breathed your last breath before receiving Christ, though your darkened soul would be living—in a sense—it would remain separated from God and the agape love he continually extended to you. Thus, your lost soul would be hopelessly mired in the torment of hell—the lake of fire—for eternity, never to be afforded eternal life. How tragic this truth is for the stubborn lost; but how glorious for you, since you asked Jesus's forgiveness and were permanently indwelled by the life-giving Holy Spirit.

The sad note is one replaced with a joyful one. You, Christian, *are filled* with life. Your lifelessness has been made alive. The river of life, as seen by the prophet Ezekiel, represents the life-filled eternal Spirit flowing into your once lost and deadened soul. The Spirit of God—the Holy Spirit—took up residence within your soul and brought teeming life in as he overcame the darkness by way of the forgiveness of Jesus, your Redeemer and Savior.

The Holy Spirit is represented by the flowing river of Ezekiel's prophecy. What was a vision at one point has become reality with you, as your soul is permanently indwelled by the Spirit of Jesus: The Holy Spirit—the Spirit of truth. From the origin of the water flowing from under the threshold of the temple of God—first ankle deep, then knee deep, followed by waist deep, and ultimately an over-the-head depth of surrounding life—your saved soul is the receptacle of God's agape love and his everlasting life. This is an awesome truth that goes beyond a one-time filling. Your soul has the capacity to be continually filled as God tells us in his Word to "be filled" (literally: "be being filled") with the Holy Spirit.

Being continually filled with the Spirit of God requires one to be an active and alive outlet of the filling. Unlike the barren Dead Sea with no outlet, each redeemed soul of Jesus becomes his outlet into the lost world. Your soul is as a sea of life teeming with the agape love of God.

This is where I would like to present to you the question, what is your depth? Your once dead and barren soul (covered by the darkness of sin) is now filled with the living and active Holy Spirit—the same Spirit who inspired the living and active Word of God. He is teeming with life—even more so than the river of Ezekiel's prophecy. You have, as a Christian living in this world, a choice. This choice is to completely accept the eternal Holy Spirit in his fullness and continued filling or to remain a saved Christian going about your daily routine of life, vulnerable to the sway of the world. Fully submerged in the Spirit *is* the place to be. And that is exactly where God desires that you be.

When you first received Jesus as Lord and Savior, there was a great power that caused your decision. Let me be clear; the great power may not have been acknowledged by you presently. You may have heard the witness of a friend, or a Sunday-morning message may have been a prompt to you. Other means of awareness are possible. You know your situation.

The key is that the great power—that which proceeded from the Father, Son, and Holy Spirit, prompted you with agape love. As the title of this book declares, it all began with love.

The River of Life, the constantly flowing stream of living water, is yours. It is because of this truth that you can make a conscionable decision. It is through the words before you, containing the truth of the Word of God, and ultimately through the guiding of the Holy Spirit permanently residing in your saved soul, that you have the choice. You can choose to remain in an ankle-deep relationship with the Lord, or you can progress and plunge headlong into the wonderful depths of the River of Life.

Recall the words of Jesus as he said in a loud voice while standing in the temple courts on the last and greatest day of the festival, "If anyone is thirsty, let him come to me and drink. Whoever believes in me, as the Scripture has said, streams of living water will flow from within him." (John 7:37b—38).

The River of Life flows in as you allow. Thus, the streams of living water will flow from within you. It all depends how deep your spirit is submerged within the Spirit of God.

You, Christian, are absolutely indwelled by the Holy Spirit. This was Jesus's promise, as is recorded in John 14. He promised his Holy Spirit to return, as would be requested of the Father. Upon his return, all who would believe would receive forgiveness of sin, as this had been paid for by the Lord Jesus, and his Spirit would immediately come into each redeemed soul. This divine fact remains true for you. The

Holy Spirit remains within your saved soul. And with this divine fact in place and active, it is up to you to decide how deep you will plunge your soul into the Spirit of God.

Your soul was once lifeless to God and now is made alive. It all began with love, and it continues with the same agape love of God! He desires that you be in his company daily. How can this happen? Read on and the best-kept secret will be unveiled.

CHAPTER 8

The Best-Kept Secret

Communication is the best-kept secret, yet it is the most obvious human ability. Everywhere we go, there is some means of communication occurring. How about beginning with some of the remotest scenes. The Vietnam war was one where communication was used as a tool of survival. Prisoners of war were huddled and crunched into ridiculously cramped cubicles to wait out their demise. It was through code that these heroes adapted a means of communication. Sanity was maintained, solace was shared, plans were made, and sharing God's Word became a saving grace.

In this current day and age, communication has become almost an obsession. Internet contact with people around the globe, at an instant click, is reality. This may not be the complete case, as there are regions of the world where people still communicate by primitive means. Chief Treeboat of the Amazon still communicates by simple methods. Other cultures of people around the globe connect to the outside world through ancient means, such as fire and smoke. With the inception of space travel, certain means of communication have been established through similar satellite technology as is currently used between Earth-dwellers. The latest craze of communication is the transmission of text messages over cell phones and related technology. This means of being in instant contact has become a helpful tool while at the same time it has turned into a nemesis. I will give a short example of the downside of this current technology.

When I was a kid personal communication, if not available by means of face-to-face contact, came by way of the telephone—this apparatus was hardwired into most homes. Should I want to have a conversation with my friend who lived down the street or on the other side of town, I would simply pick up the receiver and dial his number. If he answered the phone at his location we would communicate for a few minutes, become mutually aware of the intention of the call, make plans or reach a conclusion on a subject, etc., and end the conversation.

As you know, there are still hardwired telephones available. As a matter of fact, I have one in my office. I also have available to me a cell phone—of which I use to occasionally text. These are great tools of communication, to be sure. The downside presents itself to me by way of the myriad applications included in the cell phone technology. What used to be a tool of personal contact which was limited to certain times—such as not interrupting the family meal and the like—the new apparatuses of almost endless use have presented a problem. What used to be a practical tool of infrequent communication has evolved into a finger tapping obsession that distracts more than focuses.

The downside that I see presents itself by way of the actual loss of personal contact. The trend of 'texting' has become so overwhelming. Here is one of many examples: There are times when I am speaking face to face with a person and, out of the blue, their cell phone beeps or sings and immediately our conversation is put on hold. The person with whom I am holding a conversation instantly places me on the sideline with the raise of a finger or with a line such as, "I've got to answer this." Without one thought of being rude, the person fires off a text and then proceeds to attempt further communication with me. More times than not, the conversation is cut short because our initial thought was disrupted.

Reading this description, you may feel I'm anti-new technology. I have my reservations but I believe progress is a good thing, though moderation and common courtesy currently suffer due to lack of conscious personal consideration. Non-the-less we are God's creation and our devices of communication continue to take on new forms. Regardless whether we wrap ourselves up in the rapid pace of the current generation or enjoy a life of chosen peace, the fact remains that we have God and he desires to be in constant communication with his redeemed children in a whole-hearted way.

On the upside, whether you are an avid texter or a person who prefers some of the old-school approaches to communication, have you considered the wonderful opportunity at your complete advantage— this being the 24-7 capability of instantly communicating with God? This technology came way before the use of codes or smoke or even texting. Yes, it was around when God created the first man and woman. It was God who began communication. His Word tells us he spoke to man. He also communicated to man through visions and dreams and through his Spirit. The Bible is filled with these truths (a complete study of which would comprise much more investigation than this current work can allow).

If communication is such a sought-after means to the human being, it should occur to the race that this avenue can extend beyond the current craze of personal texting and or quickly connecting to the planets of our galaxy through signals and such.

Christian, you have the best-kept secret at the tips of your fingers, on the tip of your tongue, in the palm of your hands, and, most importantly, in your redeemed soul. The engine that drives your communication with your Creator—your agape-love God—is him. The Holy Spirit, who has been communicating with God's chosen ones through the ages, is now at your instant acknowledgment. You, through your deliberate awareness, have the same means available as does each saved one of Jesus. The Holy Spirit, who Jesus promised you and I, gives us his complete attention. He will not break communication. He hears everything you say to him. And in his uninterrupted way, he communicates with you personally. A magnificent way he does this is through the Word of God. The life of Jesus as recorded in the Gospels is a wonderful way of knowing the Holy Spirit's communication to you. His text is available to you always. In addition, the entire Bible is the Holy Spirit's tangible means of divine communication to the saved in Christ.

Keeping Jesus in mind and focusing on his flawless skill of communication, we can—by the guiding of the Holy Spirit—learn from our Lord's perfect example of prayer. This impeccable means was set in motion for us through the observation of his disciples and by their request. Jesus, according to God's Word, would rise early in the morning and go to a quiet place to communicate with the Father. Out of this beautiful example, his disciples asked Jesus to teach them how to be in contact with the Father. He taught them simply. It was through prayer—a personal means of communication with God—that his first disciples became aware of this simple though awesomely powerful and confirming means. In Section 2 of this book, Holy Spirit Power Guide Prayers, you will be invited to partake in this energizing means as you exercise your awareness and connection with the Holy Spirit through his awesome power.

This asset of praying wasn't what the disciples were accustomed to witnessing. In their day in many cases, prayer was used for show by the Pharisees, though there was genuine prayer happening around them, as is made evident in the Bible. One instance I will cite is acknowledged as honorable and is almost shadowed by obscurity. It is pointed out on the day the infant, Jesus, was taken to the temple to be dedicated to God. Listen to what the scripture tells us: "There was a prophetess, Anna, the daughter of Phanuel, of the tribe of Asher. She was very old; She had lived with her husband seven years after her marriage, and then was a widow until she was eighty-four. She never left the temple but worshipped night and day, fasting and praying. Coming up to them at that very moment, she gave thanks to God and spoke about the child to all who were looking forward to the redemption of Jerusalem" (Luke 2:36–38). This soul was quietly dedicated to genuine prayer. This is the kind of communication

God desires from you and me. The question is, how do we initiate and maintain such a reciprocating communique? Awareness of *who* indwells our spirit—our redeemed soul—is the answer. Just as we have acknowledged the Holy Spirit being represented by the river flowing from the temple of God, we also must firmly recognize him as our direct line of communication with the Father.

Jesus taught the disciples how to genuinely pray. Anna had already gotten the picture, as she prayed daily to the Father in the temple. There was an understanding that God was instantly available. This is the total first unveiling of the best-kept secret. God is available through his Conduit. His Conduit is our continual tie with the Father through the Holy Spirit, whom Jesus made available to us through his unconditional sacrifice on the cross and through his resurrection from the dead.

You, Christian, have the instant means of communication with God residing within your redeemed soul. Your spirit—soul—once disconnected from God and as good as the lifeless salt sea, has been made alive and is now divinely capable of constant communication with God. How awesome is this! New life is teeming from within, flowing like a never-ending river connecting perpetually with your Creator, Savior, and Sustainer.

The main difference between communication among man and communication with God is that, regardless of the means, communication among man is restricted. This is not the case with God. Your Line—that is, your River of Life, or your eternal indwelling Holy Spirit of God—is operational 24-7 and never goes down for repairs, updates, stoking, or anything else. You *are* connected!

No longer should this awesome reality be the best-kept secret in your Christian life. Embrace the truth. Exercise your newfound age-old fact. Communicate! Have faith! Loosen up and be actively activated through confidence in the Holy Spirit. What's the answer?

CHAPTER 9

Faith Loosens and Activates

Faith is related to confidence. The Bible tells us: "Now faith is being sure of what we hope for and certain of what we do not see" (Hebrews 11:1). Does this definition sound like faith to you? When was the last time you exercised confidence? Do you drive a vehicle? Do you walk a dog? Do you support your favorite sports team? All these things, and more, require confidence.

I should say this with caution. Some time ago I was watching a documentary on television and the subject matter was based on *lack* of confidence. As a matter of fact, it was centered on phobia. One case presented involved a young woman living in London, England. Her phobia, or lack of confidence, involved driving her car. Her lack of confidence caused her to be able to make only left turns. Taking the viewing audience through one of her courses involved driving to the grocery store. She started the car's engine and drove from her home, initiating the journey with a left-hand turn. She then proceeded forward, almost relentlessly making many left turns to successfully get to her desired location. Because of lack of confidence, or trust in her ability, the young woman went several miles out of the way to reach the store. If she had placed confidence in herself to make right-hand turns in combination with left-hand turns, her trip would have been shortened by more than half the distance. The store seemed to be but a stone's throw from her home. The documentary did not show her return trip. I can only imagine it was another drawn-out left-hand rally.

The reason I bring up the idea of confidence is that Christians are prone to lack of this quality. I am baffled by this. Being a minister, I have had opportunity from the pulpit view to observe the congregation. Many times, at the closing of the service I've asked different members to end in prayer. With some the praying flows like a stream filled with vibrant and refreshing water. On other occasions, this is not the case. Some brothers or sisters, when called upon, seem to go into a mode of panic. Their voices become almost hoarse or raspy. The looks on their faces appear to suggest they've seen a ghost. The prayers are usually very short. And after the "amen," a sense of relief slowly changes the once petrified soul. Because of the lack of confidence, I have been requested by such members that I don't call on them again. Out of respect, I honor their wishes. The fact remains that they are Christians and should be confident ambassadors of Christ.

Lack of assurance in some cases and full assurance in others forms a line. This line should never be in play. The Holy Spirit of God is powerfully in your soul and the soul of each Christian. Yes, nervousness enters the picture with all of us. For whatever reason, when playing the guitar in my music room, I'm as cool as a cucumber. On the other hand, when playing in front of a group of people, even in church, my hands drip with sweat and I force myself to play without bumbling the notes. One thing I have noticed is that whenever I play a tune a number of times over a period of weeks in front of a group, I tend not to sweat and my fingers move more fluidly. I could cop to the adage "Practice makes perfect." This may very well apply, but in communicating with the Lord, let's place our confident faith in his Spirit to be our Energizer and Guide. Let's cling to confident faith first, through the awesome power of the Holy Spirit.

We are to practice our faith through the Holy Spirit's power because he confidently indwells and fills us. While we allow the Holy Spirit to guide us as his witness of Jesus Christ to the world, either by conversation or example, we do become more confident. It is because of our faith and trust in the Holy Spirit that we flow like the stream.

I have a book in my library entitled *The Confidence Factor.* The author is Pastor Tom Mullins. He is a former football coach who developed such a notable character that still, thirty plus years later, he is referred to as "Coach." In many of his sermons, Coach makes note of football terminology, plays, and procedures. He is confident when it comes to this area and is also confident when it comes to preaching and conveying the gospel. In tandem with his life's love, football, Coach places his confident faith in the Father, Son, and Holy Spirit.

When I first acquired my copy of The Confidence Factor, I read it through without hesitation. It was exciting. Pastor Tom illustrated points about confidence that woke up my spirit concerning faith. As a coach, Coach was driven; he was driven even as a football player in his younger years. I was so inspired by the book that I purchased a dozen copies and randomly handed them to Christian brothers and sisters. His message was that we must have confidence in life and display that confidence as Christian representatives—saved ones of the Lord Jesus Christ.

Because of what Pastor Tom conveyed in his book, I felt compelled to make up small wooden boxes with the word "confidence" etched into the top. I desired to print quotations from Coach that would lie inside each box. My instruction to the recipient of the vessel would be to daily open the box and randomly choose a quote of confidence. After reading the inducement, the Christian would further be encouraged to visit God's Word and pray to him through the Holy Spirit with confidence. I believe this would be a great tool— one with which confidence could be learned through repetition.

This project is still on my list of things to do; I have yet to make such an aid. I hope to secure copyright permission to use Coach's quotes.

Have you been encouraged by the past few paragraphs? Have any ideas crossed your mind in respect to confidence? Can you identify with Coach and his evident confidence? Such inspiring Christians are good for our souls. By way of observing through their experiences, we can begin to practice what is needed to be the confident Christians we are intended to be.

Let me add one more confidence factor about Coach. His evident confidence—true faith—in God absolutely beams from his soul. Each time I've been around him, I have felt his confidence. Whether sitting with him at my dining room table or standing with him in the auditorium of his home church, the same confident spirit flows. He is truly following the example of faith we are encouraged to embrace.

Please know that we are not to be clones of other Christians. We are unique in the eyes of God. In the book, I am writing, entitled *I Am Unique*, there are things I've learned about myself that have been most eye-opening. It has been made evident to me that God made me to be me. He has blessed me to be a minister but not to follow in the footsteps of such blessed ministers as Coach or Adrian Rogers or Charles Stanley. He has made Billy Graham to be unique, as well as John Walvoord. The only thing we have in common, and this includes you, is that we were created by God. We were created by him to do good works he has prepared in advance for us to do, and to serve at his pleasure. He did not need to make two of us exactly alike. Our alikeness converges where he desires; and that is at the cross of Christ and in his eternal life, as was ushered into each of us by the Holy Spirit.

This is where faith comes in. Confidence is one thing. Faith is another. Though both can and do work hand in hand, faith outranks the former. It is through confidence that God blesses us to continue to do a work he calls us into by way of being proficient—such as the professionalism Pastor Tom, Coach, acquired through practice over the years. Faith is that which we possess before the confidence begins to be borne in our Christian life.

The title of this chapter is "Faith Loosens and Activates." Because of the initial occurrence of faith, the Christian, by the guiding of the Holy Spirit, becomes loose—such as to intimidation felt when asked on the spot to pray out loud. Once loose, the activation kicks in.

Allow me to illustrate from a personal experience. I was called by the Lord to preach at an early age. I was eight. You may be smiling at this point. That's okay; I know the Lord spoke to my heart because of what I was watching on my grandmother's black-and-white TV set. It was back when we received only two local channels. The pictures were mostly fuzzy. That day I chose the clearer of the two. There was a preacher by the name of Billy Graham on the other side of the glass tube. He was preaching a blue streak, and my heart was filled with excitement. If you were to ask me what he was preaching that day, I wouldn't be able to tell you. I was enamored by what the Lord was doing through him. That is what I *do* remember.

It was as if I felt the hand of God reach out of that TV screen and touch my heart while I heard the words "This is what I want you to do." Even as I sit here typing these words, I sense the awesomeness I felt way back then. I could have discounted the whole thing. God had different plans. It was always somewhere in my heart that I would serve the Lord in the capacity of a minister. Many different turns occurred in my life as a Christian. After thirty-two years of following the path I knew the Lord was leading me on, one bright Sunday morning made the difference that would change my life forever.

It was the guiding of the Holy Spirit, to whom I had yet to be formally introduced, that brought me to that point in time. That journey, which began years ago, was freshly begun on a brand-new day. To make a long story short, the scene began in a local church—one on whose threshold I had never set foot. From the moment, my wife and daughter and I entered until the moment we left, I knew *that ground* was where God was going to begin the work he had prepared in advance and had called me into thirty-two years prior.

The Spirit of God took the faith I had and loosened it into active working. The local church God instructed me to visit that morning became our church for seven years. I spent those years in the mentorship of God's appointed pastor. Pastor Terry faithfully guided me in instruction, and eventually the call of the Lord was acknowledged by my ordination. I was a minister of the Word of God. And I still am today.

During my early days of ministry, many unnerving times accompanied this Christian soul. To single out one would illustrate my point that faith loosens and activates. I was called on to preach the gospel for the first time. I was not ordained at that point. Pastor Terry wanted me to get my feet wet. And that I did. I was so tense that my nerves were tighter than Uncle Johnny's hat band. I believe the word "loose" was not in my vocabulary. Stepping up to the pulpit, I was so jittery that I felt as if I were going to be sick. Oddly enough, the message I had prepared was based on faith. I had drawn the theme from the letter of James: "But someone will say, 'You have faith; I have deeds.' Show me your faith without deeds, and I will show you my faith by what I do" (James 2: 18).

I remember asking Jesus to help me deliver the message without bumbling as I looked upon the congregation. He allowed me to bumble a bit. After a strained sentence or two, I felt as if I had been released from a tight-jawed vise. At that moment, I could see as if there were words before me explaining faith and action. The sermon that poured forth was one of excitement. It was as if I were sharing absolute joy with the congregation. I remember Pastor Terry, who was sitting in the front row, saying in an excited, tremulous voice, "Preach it, brother!"

As I write these words, I feel chills all over. The excitement of that moment is revisiting my soul. I was loosened and activated. It was the Holy Spirit who did it. I called upon Jesus for help, and he absolutely delivered through the Holy Spirit I knew but just a trifle about.

From that day forward, I knew the truth the Lord had laid on my heart in my grandmother's living room: "This is what I want you to do." I put my hand to the plow and never looked back. Faith had loosened and activated my soul. The Holy Spirit was at work, and he has continued to excite me even to the point of writing this book, *Yes! It All Began with Love*, for you to know the same divine truth and excitement, as well as how important he is in your redeemed life.

That day at the pulpit, I was connected and energized. It was so awesome and continues to actively remain to this day! Faith put into practice has evidenced the first sermon I ever preached. To God be the glory!

Confidence is a product of faith unabated. "Faith is being sure of what we hope for and certain of what we do not see." Faith loosens and activates.

Will you allow the Holy Spirit to guide you into active faith as you exercise confidence? Come with me, and we will see what it is, through faith, to *allow* and *bear.*

CHAPTER 10

Allowing Is Great—Bearing Is Greater

Christian, you have now been introduced to the Holy Spirit. You are aware of the ultimate reason God put him into your soul. Agape love is where it all began. You know that Jesus went to the cross to die for your sin, which separated you from fellowship with your Creator, God. The forgiveness Jesus purchased while upon the cross made it possible for you to become one of his saved children brought back into full fellowship with God the Father. His resurrection from the dead ultimately made way for your eternal life with him, as your redeemed spirit was connected with the Holy Spirit the moment you received Jesus as your Lord and Savior; and this was an instantaneous act of God the Father. You are a forgiven, born again, Holy Spirit–indwelled, eternally baptized child of God. Your redeemed soul is covered over by the righteous cleansing blood of Jesus, and your soul is sealed by the Holy Spirit. You are indeed a full member of the body of Christ.

Now that this truth has been revealed to you, and you have accepted this truth by faith, it is time for you to become aware of the Gift within you and the fruit he will produce through you.

To reiterate, before Jesus went to the cross, he made an eternal promise. It was made in the hearing of eleven disciples. At Jesus's command the betrayer, Judas Iscariot, had already left the company to make plans with the accusers to arrest Jesus later that night. After the Lord brought the disciples into the awareness of the promised gift of the Holy Spirit, Jesus informed the disciples further of what would happen upon receiving the Holy Spirit.

Be reminded that the promise to the disciples was one made also to whosoever would believe. You are one of the "whosoever believers" now sharing the eternal Gift of the Holy Spirit. With this in mind, picture yourself in the hearing of Jesus at the Passover table. The eleven are gathered around the table, and Jesus begins to speak to each one individually, including you. "I am the true vine, and my Father is the gardener ... Remain in me, and I will remain in you. No branch can bear fruit by itself; it must remain in the vine. Neither can you bear fruit unless you remain in me. I am the vine; you are the branches. If a man remains in me and I in him, he will bear much fruit; apart from me you can do nothing" (John 15:1, 4–5).

The crux of the matter working within is faithful inclusion. Every redeemed soul has a responsibility to Jesus Christ through the indwelling Holy Spirit. Jesus made it known he is the true vine. He also confirmed the Father is the gardener. The gardener prunes the branches as they grow in order that they will bear lasting fruit. This is found in John 15:2.

Here a very important point is being made. What Jesus is bringing into the forefront is the fact of the unified working of the Father, the Son, and the Holy Spirit. Charles Stanley made an outstanding observation in his book *The Wonderful Spirit-Filled Life*.

Fresh out of seminary, Pastor Stanley was new to the pastoral ministry. During this time, he was called upon to teach a class to pastors on the subject of the Holy Spirit. Charles cautiously accepted. As the day for the class to begin grew closer, the young Pastor Stanley was in great distress. He was clueless. He had read book after book on the subject and prayed a ton of prayers. The night before the class was to begin, the perplexed minister knelt before God and begged for mercy. He was not prepared to face the well-seasoned pastors scheduled to assemble in his classroom. He knew he was going to miserably fail. God had another plan. That night God led Charles right back to the passage I just shared with you. The focus was on "I am the vine; you are the branches. If a man remains in me and I in him, he will bear much fruit; apart from me you can do nothing."

This revelation became a lifetime fulfillment for Pastor Stanley. The initial unveiling came to him by way of viewing Jesus as the vine. Followed by the vine, he envisioned the branches. He also saw the result of the branches being connected to the vine—namely, the fruit. One thing God revealed to the pastor was the inside of the vine, the branches, and the fruit. It was the lifeblood. That would be none other than the Holy Spirit, as represented by the *sap*. Unless the sap flows through the vine, there is no life. It was a divine eureka moment! The stage was set for Pastor Stanley, and the course was a success. Thus, Pastor Stanley has been teaching his congregation and millions of others about the Father, Son, and Holy Spirit as related to Jesus's instruction to the first disciples. And this is one of many thousands of subjects he has faithfully conveyed through the guiding of the Holy Spirit.

The revelation given to Charles Stanley is one that widely opened my eyes to the flowing of the Holy Spirit in my life. I was a new pastor when I acquired his book, and I have gleaned valuable information in accompaniment with God's Word. Of late, during my recovery period from the heart repair, the Lord has given me a new perspective on the Holy Spirit and the message I should convey to the Christian. Charles Stanley's book has been used of the Lord to illuminate yet another important Holy Spirit–related work.

Jesus tells us we are to bear fruit. What caught my attention in Stanley's book, which I have read numerous times, was the difference between bearing and producing. Plain and simple, just as the Lord revealed to the young minister the need for the lifeblood, the sap, it is important to understand the difference between producing and bearing.

Are you producing fruit as Jesus is expecting of you? Try as you might in your Christian walk, it is impossible for you to *produce* fruit. The simple answer is that the Father, Son, and Holy Spirit are responsible for producing the fruit. With this being said, is your fruit evident to others? You may answer with "I don't know" or possibly "I don't know what fruit I'm supposed to be displaying." Believe it or not, there are large numbers of Christians who don't know what fruit I'm asking about. Awareness of the Holy Spirit is one thing, but knowing him as the producer of the fruit you are to bear, and the kind of that fruit, is another.

The title of this chapter is "Allowing Is Great; Bearing Is Greater." The original intention of *Yes! It All Began with Love* was that all Christians be made aware of the importance of the Holy Spirit in our lives. The preceding pages have introduced and invited you to the Holy Spirit indwelling your redeemed soul. I pray you now have a better understanding of the Spirit of God. Because of this introduction and invitation, you have been given the opportunity to allow the Holy Spirit to become more evident to you, a Christian. This truth is of vital importance and is not to be downplayed. Great is great! In God's sight, *greater* only builds upon or enhances *great*. In the same way, when you allow the Holy Spirit to fully function in your Christian life, this is great. In addition to this, when you allow the Holy Spirit to produce lasting fruit through you, this is greater. He is at full throttle when you are bearing the fruit Jesus has told us to bear.

Are you curious about what fruit the Holy Spirit is producing in your redeemed soul? Picture the true vine, the branches, the fruit, and the lifeblood. A picture is worth a thousand words. Let's step into the divine vineyard.

CHAPTER 11

Preparing the Fruit

It's one thing as a Christian to know the Holy Spirit exists within your soul. It's quite another to be acquainted with him to the point of bearing the fruit Jesus said we must bear. At the onset of *Yes! It All Began with Love*, I made it clear that the immense love of God is the reason the Holy Spirit is in permanent residence within your saved soul. You were also made aware that the Father loved Jesus before the creation of the world, thus making clear that the Father's love has no beginning or end.

As we step into the divine vineyard, it is important we allow our eyes to be further opened as to our being here in the first place. Looking at it from the perspective of the Father loving Jesus before the creation of the world, let's focus on that agape love Jesus displayed while he was on this earth. There is no better tangible example of the love of God than Jesus himself. The only begotten Son sent to us by the Father is our perfect example of agape love—the perfect fruit. It is precisely this love that Jesus sets before us as the divinely produced fruit we are to bear. It is the Holy Spirit Jesus promised us and delivered who produces Jesus's love within us. It is also the Holy Spirit who works through us so that we will bear the fruit of love—the fruit that will last.

Through the inspiration of the Spirit of truth—the Spirit of Jesus, the Holy Spirit—the apostle Paul conveyed to the Galatians in his letter the pureness of the essence of the Holy Spirit actively present within our souls. Here's what is recorded in God's Word: "But the fruit of the Spirit is love, joy, peace, patience, kindness, goodness, faithfulness, gentleness, and self-control. Against such things there is no law. Those who belong to Christ have crucified the sinful nature with its passions and desires. Since we live by the Spirit, let us keep in step with the Spirit. Let us not become conceited, provoking and envying each other" (Galatians 5:22–26).

Before we approach the true vine that we may embrace the main ingredient of the fruit of the Spirit, let's look at a few important things we as Christians are commanded to do in order that the agape love of God will flow through us as we will bear the lasting fruit. To be on the right page of fruit-bearing, it is crucial that we know where the rubber meets the road. As we are warned in Paul's message which unveils the fruit of the Spirit, we are to be aware of our position as saved Christians. Being in such a state, we are representatives of Jesus Christ in this world. There are worldly influences nipping at our heels daily. Therefore, it is important for us to realize the power within us. This power—the Holy Spirit—is there for our good and for the glory of God. Representing Jesus means honoring who he is as the glorified Christ and our Redeemer—the true vine.

When you made the conscious determination to accept Jesus as Lord and Savior, you were serious about this decision. It was the most important move you've made in your entire life. In the witness of the Father, Son, and Holy Spirit, your acceptance of the forgiveness of Jesus was paramount, and your name was entered into the book of life. Thus, you are a branch of the true vine. This is a very serious matter. This is where the Holy Spirit becomes significant in your life as a Christian. It cannot be taken lightly that you chose to become Christ's own. By freely making this conscious choice, you came into full agreement with Christ Jesus. He became your perfect example from that point and remains so eternally. You are abiding in Jesus, and he is abiding in you.

Now take a further step into the picture of the divine vineyard. Focus on the true vine. Can you see the branches attached to the vine? You *are* one of the attached branches. Your attachment proves you belong to Jesus, your Savior. He is the one who paid the highest price for the redemption of your once sin-darkened soul. He is the one who gave the order to remain in him—the true vine—and to continually abide in him. By doing so, you will bear pure fruit—the fruit of the Spirit—and this is lasting fruit. Any fruit borne by you that is not of the Spirit will certainly perish and will in essence become a stench in the nostrils of the Father.

Hear what the Holy Spirit is saying to you through Paul: "Since we live by the Spirit, let us keep in step with the Spirit." This is clearly the direction the Father commands us to follow and also spotlights the path Jesus blazed for us out of his unconditional love for you and me.

Look for a moment, if you will, from the perspective of the vine and the branches. Consider these as being the unrestricted path Jesus blazed. The highway of your life is clearly laid out for your Christian walk. Let's go a bit deeper into the subject. Picture yourself inside the vine (being reminded of what Jesus tells us: "remain in me and I will remain in you"). Being in the vine, you are encompassed by the purity of God and enveloped and illuminated with his agape love. You are one of the many branches growing and flourishing as part of the vine. Originating inside the vine, and freely flowing through the branches, is the lifeblood.

Now flash back to the Ezekiel prophecy and recall the flowing river of life. The desire of God is that you choose to be fully submerged in the river, thus representing yourself as being completely committed to him. Apply this to your current journey within the vine and the branches. The maximum flow of the lifeblood is undoubtedly within the vine and is all-encompassing. It's not ankle deep or knee deep or waist deep; it's over the head and is consuming. It fills the vine and branches to full capacity, providing full potential for your excellent lasting fruit-bearing.

While taking in the awesomeness of the moment, let's look at another aspect of the vine and the branches while including the lifeblood and your involvement in the picture. Allow, once again, the Holy Spirit to speak to you through Paul as he finalizes the current declaration of the subject concerning the fruit of the Spirit. The last verse is a warning and a caution. "Let us not become conceited, provoking and envying each other." This caution and warning is just as relevant today as it was the day Paul penned the letter to the Galatians. For a Christian to bear quality, lasting fruit, he or she must be fully committed. Conceit, provoking and envy unfortunately cause restriction of the full flow of the lifeblood. Likewise, any lack of your full commitment to the Lord causes restriction of flow of the lifeblood. Inside the vine and branches, set yourself in the branch that is actually yourself—your saved soul. Sure enough, you have the lifeblood within. Is your pathway—the branch—unrestricted and free flowing with the lifeblood or have you allowed conceit or envy or provoking or any other number of offenses to form an obstruction thus restricting the Holy Spirit's lifeblood to fully flow?

I again refer to my heart attack as an illustration. The instant illness was due to arteries that had, over time, become severely blocked. Cholesterol was a key factor in the blockages. Had I known a problem existed, I would have visited the doctor for a checkup. Thinking I was in good condition, which I was on the outside, I continued through daily life. At the end of the day, my heart was failing to produce the proper blood flow necessary to sustain a healthy body. In other words, the flow was restricted to the point of my body dying; good fruit, if you will, was not being borne. Blood was entering in at a full flow but was being restricted by the clogged branches.

In the case of you, the branch, whether the full flow of the lifeblood is allowed in is up to you, the Christian. A trickle or a flood is allowed by you to happen. Taking it a step further, see yourself in the picture as the fruit. The flow of the lifeblood is severely restricted.

The inside of the fruit is showing signs of death and decay—not a very healthy scene. It is obvious the fruit is in poor health because of the restricted flow of the lifeblood.

This is a sad scenario in the case of many Christians today. Restricting the Holy Spirit causes lack of flow within and stymies his work he produces through you. The fruit, Jesus orders the redeemed to bear, is not at this point of high quality, because of issues that have been allowed to leak into the Christian life.

Where do you stand as far as this picture is concerned? I can assure you that there are no perfect Christians. Jesus knows this full well. Though it is true, this is not to be a cop-out for any of us. The bottom line is that the restricted flow can be divinely worked out.

A problem Paul saw in the Galatian group was conceit, provocation, and envy. Instead of being guided by the Spirit of God to the fullest extent, these folks were allowing the sway of the world to get in and destroy. Paul was warning and cautioning against what was plaguing the saved souls.

Whether it be envy, deceit, provocation, or any number of decaying distractions of the world, it is up to you and me and every Christian to fully submit to the guiding of the Holy Spirit— the lifeblood. Jesus tells us that the Holy Spirit—the Spirit of truth—will guide us into all truth. Through faith, cheerfully and confidently submitting to this call of God, we stand to have better lifeblood flowing from within so the fruit produced by the Holy Spirit from within our redeemed souls will enable us to bear fruit that will last, thus making the branches healthy fruit bearers of the lasting fruit produced from the true vine as the lifeblood freely flows. This is a beautiful picture indeed! And more beautifully, it brings glory to God the Father, God the Son, and God the Holy Spirit!

Stepping out of the scene of the divine vineyard, let's open our hearts to the Holy Spirit as he guides us, as willing Christians, into the blessing of bearing fruit that will last—lasting fruit that will be borne inwardly, God-wardly, and outwardly.

CHAPTER 12

Bearing Lasting Fruit

Once again because of my downtime, the Lord opened my eyes to the fruit of the Spirit, of which I had not previously taken notice. It was through Billy Graham's book *The Holy Spirit* that I was given a beautiful picture of the fruit and was, through my mind's-eye view, led by the Holy Spirit to focus on the perfect fruit demonstrated by our Lord and Savior, Jesus Christ—that very same fruit we divinely have within by way of the eternally residing Holy Spirit.

Being originally from the state of Georgia, I tend to like peaches. I mean tasty farm-fresh peaches! You may ask, "How do farm-fresh peaches relate to the fruit of the Spirit or the agape love of God?" A sweet savory taste always tends to make an impression. Likewise, a sweet savory fruit of the Spirit that the Christian bears for Christ through the agape love of God the Father leaves a significant lasting impression.

A healthy peach tree will produce excellent peaches that will be collected and distributed to satisfied consumers. Would you agree that a Christian committed to Jesus, the epitome of the agape love of God the Father, and who is consciously aware of the indwelling of the Holy Spirit within, would also be the vehicle of sweet savory fruit produced by God? This Christian, a blessed vehicle of the Lord, indeed, is a bearer of lasting fruit. His or her lasting fruit borne in honor of the Lord is pleasantly experienced by satisfied Christians

and is as well enjoyed as delicious fruits of witness, ripe for the picking, to be pleasantly consumed by the world?

The above is God's desire for every Christian. It would be a glorious scene should every Christian bear such savory fruit for Jesus. The world would be such a different place. God would be honored in great degree. The sacrifice of Jesus would be recognized by so many that discord would be in danger of distinction. Unfortunately, in this day and age, much adversity exists and Christians are hard-pressed to bear the lasting and savory fruit of the Spirit for Christ Jesus. Though this is sadly true in many cases, God will not give up on his own. The Holy Spirit is untiringly answering the call. It is through the perfect example of Jesus that the Holy Spirit excels while leading into all truth you and me and every willing Christian to be the fruit bearers we are called to be. One by one the Spirit of Jesus will move us from adversity and turn us to our King of kings and Lord of lords.

By truly recognizing the Holy Spirit Jesus promised every believer, and coming to a better understanding of his presence within our redeemed lives, we can become excellent fruit-bearers for the Lord. It is through the perfect example of Jesus that we learn the who, what, when, where, why, and how of this vital gift.

Each Christian is different and the Lord knows exactly where we are in our walk with him. As we continue our journey let's allow the Lord to point out to each of us privately, where we are individually. By taking this approach, our separate thoughts and attention give concentrated focus to *the* perfect example—Jesus. It is from his practical demonstration, as we sit at the feet of our Savior, that we Christians, one and all, can be divinely instructed while faithfully practicing the fine art of fruit-bearing.

Jesus's savory freshness seems to me to be more inviting than can be searched out through complicated explanation. Life is difficult enough without trying to matter-of-factly dissect, diagnose, and conclude what type of fruit we are expected to bear through our own self-acquired understanding. Jesus is, without a doubt, the perfect illustration and the best example to be observed and followed.

Reading through the Gospels, it is plain to see the example Jesus sets. He was always up to the task whether the scene involved people who were seeking his advice or, at other times, while he was being dogged by opposition; inclusive of the former, there are many occasions and instances recorded wherein the evidence proves his wonderful gift of Holy Spirit-blessed fruit-bearing. The Master was equipped to perfectly deal with each situation while bearing lasting fruit.

Jesus always spoke the truth. The gospels display Jesus's outstanding love in such examples as: that of the conversation he had with the Samaritan woman at the well; his encounter with the man born blind showing a compassion second to none. His teaching of the beatitudes is also a great example of laying out the fruit of the Spirit in such an inviting way that his every word was sweet and savory, truth-filled and love-laced.

Even in cases that involved rebuke, such as those where the Pharisees would corner Jesus to trap him in what they thought would prove him to be a blasphemer, he displayed the pure and lasting fruit of the Spirit.

It is in our best interest as Christians to use Jesus as the perfect example. While viewing the spiritual fruit we are to bear through *the true vine*, it behooves us, *the branches*, to consciously bear the quality, lasting fruit from its original source—and that being Jesus himself. This brings to my mind: WWJD—What Would Jesus Do.

Keeping in view the natural peach, do you believe we Christians are to bear such a fruit as that which has been altered from its original source? In today's agricultural technology, crossbreeding is something that is done to achieve certain goals. Great thought and expertise is put into these processes and proves to be beneficial in many cases. Scores of delicious fruits have come forth due to this method of engineering. This process may be acceptable in the producing and bearing of fruit we eat, but we must take a good hard look at what we, as redeemed ones of Christ, should be cautious of when it comes to bearing the lasting fruit Jesus expects us to bear. We are not to take it upon ourselves to manipulate the perfect fruit already being produced within us that is ours to obediently and cheerfully bear for our Lord and Savior.

The type of lasting fruit we are to bear for Jesus is that which the Holy Spirit possesses and produces through us as his witness to the world and his affirmation of our being saved ones of Christ the Lord. With this thought in mind, at the end of the day, what reflection would *our own* brand of fruit-bearing have on the Father, Son and Holy Spirit? That of a sweet savory fruit sought by all, or one that falls short of making a lasting pleasant impression?

Is it our place to decide what quality or mix of fruit we are to bear for Jesus other than that which he requires? Because of joyfully accepting Jesus's personal invitation which came to fruition the moment he was accepted as Lord and Savior, the Christian man or woman consciously surrendered to the will of the Father through the sacrifice of Jesus and to the continuing work of the Holy Spirit. In so doing, the new Christian cheerfully embarked upon the path that has been laid out. It is up to the Christian, through the guiding of the Holy Spirit, to follow God's plan of love.

Unfortunately, there is a disobedient alternative at hand. The Christian can choose to veer from the true path and meet with all kinds of confusion. The question is: What's the beneficial path to follow?

Christian, as I mentioned above, allow the Lord to walk with you along the path he has laid out. Allow him to personally speak to you throughout the journey. His perfect example illuminated by the Holy Spirit will bring to light your part in being a *branch* of *the true vine.* He is the vine, you are *one* of his branches and the Holy Spirit is the lifeblood flowing within. There is no combination better assembled wherein you can be a cheerful fruit-bearer of sweet and savory lasting fruit for Jesus.

Now, let's step further into the picture and see how the agape love of God enhances the sweet savor of his fruit produced by Jesus through the working of the Holy Spirit—powered by the love that began it all—**the most excellent way.**

CHAPTER 13

The Most Excellent Way

In the opening of *Yes! It All Began with Love,* we discovered God's reason for our existence. His love is so deep for us! His love is the most excellent way. Let's take a step into the First Letter of Paul to the Corinthians. The intention is to focus on the love of God being the source of lasting fruit we are to joyfully bear. This love Paul describes is fruit to be borne happily in the name of Jesus and shared as we represent him.

> And now I will show you the most excellent way. (1 Corinthians 12:31)

> Love is patient, love is kind. It does not envy, it does not boast, it is not proud. It is not rude, it is not self-seeking, it is not easily angered, it keeps no record of wrongs. Love does not delight in evil but rejoices with truth. It always protects, always trusts, always hopes, always perseveres. Love never fails. (1 Corinthians 13:4–8)

Can you see, from your heart's view, the truth of love? Now that you have had time to allow God's love for you to excite your redeemed soul, do you see the root source of the fruit you are to bear for Christ Jesus? The love of God is absolutely pure and preexistent to everything. There has been no adulteration added and no essence subtracted. His love residing in your soul is the Holy Spirit, and the first recognized fruit of the Sprit is love. Every ounce of the fruit of the Spirit proceeds from the perfect agape love of God.

From time to time I've heard it preached that love, the first fruit mentioned regarding the Spirit, is that upon which, and from where, the other eight fruits of the Spirit naturally, though divinely, flow. Through my studies over the years and my examinations of various opinions, I have found evidence through the guiding of the Holy Spirit that love does lead out and shows excellent quality. The most excellent way—love—obviously encompasses the other eight fruits. Love is our origin. God is our Creator. God is love. If he is the source of our being and we come forth from his existence, then it makes perfect sense that love precedes the other fruits we are to bear, as we are centered in love. The Holy Spirit himself inspired Paul to pen the verse "And now I will show you the most excellent way." This most excellent way leads to joy, peace, patience, kindness, goodness, faithfulness, gentleness, and self-control. Without the presence—the Source—of love, none of the other fruits would be truly possible.

In his book *The Holy Spirit*, Billy Graham brings up an interesting thought to which the Lord further opened my eyes. Because of what a preacher said in relation to the fruit of the Spirit, Billy saw a correlation with the nine fruits as placed in three categories. I believe this concept does apply. I also believe that love encompasses each fruit and makes all come alive with the agape love of God. The first grouping suggests inwardness; the second, God-wardness; and the third, outwardness.

The inward fruit Jesus expects us to bear is best borne through his perfect example. Love, joy, and peace were definite inward examples of our Savior. He was no stranger to the fruit of the Spirit, whether separated into categories, singly demonstrated, or corporately combined. It is through Jesus that we not only witness through the recorded Word but we also, through ourselves, follow his perfect lead. It is the same Holy Spirit Jesus had within him who guides and empowers you and me to be bearers of lasting fruit.

Look at the outstanding inward love Jesus demonstrated in one of many instances. The crippled man at the Pool of Bethesda comes to mind. This man tried for years to get to the water when it stirred. To no avail were his attempts to enter for the healing he so desired. Jesus approached him and asked one question: "Wilt thou be healed?" The man was quick to state no one would help him into the water at the opportune moment. There was no further discussion. Jesus's display of inward love did not come by way of dipping the man's big toe into the pool. It came by heart-drenched audible means. "Then Jesus said to him, Get up! Pick up your mat and walk." Think of the love, joy, and peace Jesus knew. At that moment, his heavenly trio of fruit engulfed the once crippled man as he stood upright, carrying his mat, which had been his prison bed for so many years. Yes! From inside comes the fruit produced by the Holy Spirit; and you and I are cheerful bearers of it—If we choose to be.

This was a miracle for sure, but on the other hand, how many inward opportunities do we have on a daily basis to demonstrate the love of the Spirit through heart-drenched means? The evening before I was to go in for bypass surgery, the surgeon came into my room. The look on his face told me he had something on his mind. My first thought was, *I must be sicker than I was originally informed.* Though this was a deep-down concern, I trusted the Lord, no matter the news. The doctor cautiously asked me if I would consider giving up my scheduled time of surgery. He added that a man who was on the verge of dying needed immediate attention and asked if I would mind allowing the man to be operated on first. This probably sounds to you like a no-brainer, and you might think the doctor should have ignored me and done the work. The thing is that I had been put off one other time, and the doctor didn't want me to be agitated because my heart was already in bad enough shape. To make a long story short, I immediately told the doctor to operate on the man in pressing need. There was no recoil on my part. I felt the peace of God—his absolute love. I knew the Holy Spirit guided me to this peace-filled decision.

The look on the doctor's face was one of wonderment. I told him to have peace because the Lord had given it to me; now I was sharing it and would be praying for him and the man. Not another word was exchanged between us. He walked out of the room with a peaceful look on his earlier concerned face. The love of God was shared from a definite inward way. I believe the fruit of love (and all the rest) was borne that evening. The man did, in fact, survive. His wife and daughter were in the waiting room the next morning, and Elaine had an opportunity to audibly bear fruit for Christ as she comforted and ministered to the man's wife and daughter. The joy on Elaine's heart was poured out to a very perplexed wife and daughter. This was savory fruit indeed. God is good! God *is love!*

Allow the Holy Spirit to settle into your heart and excite you at the same time. Think of situations, minor and major, you have been in where you have had the opportunity to bear the excellent fruits of love, joy, and peace. At the same time you are allowing the Holy Spirit to remind you of these times, also look at the seriousness of his presence in your redeemed life. The day you accepted Jesus as Lord and Savior, you not only received the Holy Spirit as your Guide, Counselor, and Comforter but you also accepted Jesus's command to bear lasting fruit. You may not have grasped this truth immediately in that moment but the Spirit of Jesus—the Holy Spirit—has continually revealed this to you.

Even now as you read this book, it is important you know that the Word of God is paramount in your understanding and demonstration of the excellent love of God as you bear lasting fruit for Jesus through the power of the Holy Spirit. What a magnificent truth! The most excellent way has been at work in your redeemed soul since the first moment Christ saved you. And it is eternally confirmed in his Word. The lasting fruit you bear for Jesus is that which not only comes from within but also is demonstrated for others to enjoy.

With the fruit of the Spirit now in front of us, I would like to bring into view a very important point that has been the drive of this entire work. As has been the original idea, the purpose of this book is to introduce you, a Christian, to the Holy Spirit residing in your redeemed soul—and he is doing so out of unconditional love. The entire reason for this writing was spawned through years of sharing the gospel with the congregation. As I learned the importance of the Holy Spirit in my own life, the need to share this reality with fellow brothers and sisters in Christ became more and more apparent to me. At first The Holy Spirit revealed to me my own need of his awareness from within. Because of this and the research the Holy Spirit has led me through (and still is leading me through), I am not only excited to share him with every Christian, but I also remain compelled to do so because I can see a need crying out from individual children of God. We Christians, every one, need "the most excellent way." And this way of love is found in the Word of God.

The unfortunate reality is that a vast number of Christians don't take the time to open the pages of scripture on a regular basis, thus leaving a huge gap between their understanding of God's plan and their actual position as saved, Holy Spirit—indwelled, fruit-bearing believers in Christ.

I remain enthusiastic in this endeavor. The most excellent way is what brought me to the realization of the reason I am compelled to share these pages with you, my brother or sister in Christ. It is this most excellent way that defines the extreme need for each and every one of us to embrace completely the agape love of God. I pray the Holy Spirit will not only guide me to continue to lay down the truth through the remaining pages of this writing, but also, and very importantly, that he will guide you into understanding what he will do while faithfully producing the excellent fruit you bear as lasting fruit for Jesus, through Jesus's perfect example, thereby exciting you to increase your awareness of the Father, Son, and Holy Spirit through your daily reading of the Bible.

In all sincerity, approaching the crux of the fruit of the Spirit and keeping God's agape love in focus, tune in the Holy Spirit as he reveals to you the fruits you, a redeemed one of Christ, are expected to bear—fruits that are bathed, embellished, and savored in this first and most excellent fruit: love—agape love.

CHAPTER 14

Joy

Love, joy, and peace are fruits borne by the Christian through Jesus's perfect example. These three fruits are seen as being inward. It isn't difficult to identify these three fruits of the Spirit as those borne from within the heart and also displayed outside the Christian, which is actually the case with all the fruits. The more the Bible is read and examined, the more it becomes evident that love, joy, and peace are easily identified as generating within the heart first and then being lovingly carried out.

I have found that reading the Gospels frequently further enhances the fact that Jesus was the perfect example setter of joy and all the lasting fruits. I suggest that you take advantage of the truth of the Word of God and read, with frequency, the life of Christ. The Holy Spirit will reveal to you joy you can daily experience through the actions of Jesus. Please understand that everything Jesus did was out of truth. Whether speaking a kind word, sharing bread, or offering a sip of water, his actions were done with pure joy. The joy flowed like a river from within his heart.

Did you wake up with joy on your heart this morning? It seems some comments we hear once remain in our memories. I remember one Sunday morning on which a preacher opened his sermon, based on joy, with the question "When you get up in the morning, do you immediately say, 'Good morning, Lord!' or 'Good Lord, it's morning!?'" The congregation, myself included, got a chuckle out of the quip. It was indeed funny. On the other hand, it made perfect sense even before the preacher spoke the first word concerning the intended subject. As a matter of fact, I've preceded a sermon with the very same quip. It is definitely an attention-getter. Even though the question may indicate what could be disrespect to the Lord, I believe he has a sense of humor. (I shall be very careful with this idea.)

In all seriousness, we are talking bearing lasting fruit. Take a look at the quip while you are rubbing the sleep from your slumbering eyes. Your sight may be a bit out of focus, but nonetheless you are in the reality of stepping into the light of a brand-new day. As you toss the covers from your warm body and slide off the comfort of your bed, you have a clear opportunity to meet the day with an attitude or greet it with joy. We've all been on both sides. There are times we could stay in bed all day and forget it happened, let alone partake in its pain. On other occasions, we can't wait to fly out of the sack and plunge in headfirst to enjoy its pleasure.

What's the key? What example do we see of Christ, even as he entered a brand-new day? The Gospels tell us the Lord rose early in the morning and went to a quiet place to pray. He greeted his Father with a joyful heart. This is a beautiful example of inward joy. You may ask, "What about the night Jesus went to the garden to pray to the Father?" I could be technical and split hairs by objecting, saying that was at night. I won't be so silly as to do this. The example of Jesus's joy can be followed morning, noon, and night. He was perplexed while in prayer to the Father that night. He knew he had come to the fullness of time where the Father's will and command would be completed. And he would be the one shouldering the ultimate task. During Jesus's perplexity, his Father sent an angel to strengthen him. Jesus's own sincere words prayed to the Father clearly stated, "Not my will, but thine be done."

The key was not the sorrow Jesus felt because of the nearing event. It was the fact that he knew, without a doubt—and this knowledge coming from within or inwardly—that the Lord Jesus would follow through with the greatest of tasks and it would be embellished with joy, no matter the pain. This is the extreme example of perfect joy. No more perfect example of the fruit of joy could be displayed. His joy was, in fact, made complete.

With this in mind, look at your own life. I joked about your sleep-filled eyes struggling to meet and greet the day. We've visited Jesus in the joy of praying to the Father early in the morning and also praying while in agony. The bottom line is *joy*. Where do you stand in the daily occurrence of joy in your Christian life? Are your thoughts and emotions swayed by the world, or are you looking toward your Savior and his Spirit residing within your soul? Who has more power, the world and its magnetic sway, or your Lord with his eternal draw? It is completely up to you to decide your position. It is absolute truth that your Savior and Sustainer has the most excellent plan. Saturated in love, the fruit of joy is at your fingertips. You can either bear it as lasting fruit or diminish it before you bear it when it is no longer first quality. What do you desire? As I mentioned earlier, there are no perfect Christians. Our only perfect example—who, by the way, is beaming with joy within you and also from his throne in heaven as the glorified Christ—remains faithfully the true vine. You are eternally attached to the true vine as one of the branches. It is through the true vine that you receive his perfection. Don't forget that though your earthly flesh will remain imperfect, your redeemed soul—now the residence of the Holy Spirit—has been made perfect before the Father by the shed blood of Jesus the Son. All in all, there is perfection, and the more the Christian understands and puts this divine fact into practice, the more fruit of joy will be borne for Jesus through the power of the Holy Spirit.

This fruit indeed can be seen being borne from within. The Christian can clearly come to an understanding of the agape love of God residing within his or her soul and the fruit of joy being produced by the Holy Spirit for you to freely, cheerfully, and joyfully bear by way of faithful belief. This faithful belief opens the door to countless opportunities to share Jesus's love through the Spirit as you bear his beautiful lasting fruit of joy.

Today, who will be your first recipient of your borne fruit of joy as it wells up from within to be brilliantly shining, savory and pleasing ?

CHAPTER 15

Peace

Peace—can you think of any other way it can truly come from the Christian other than from within? Once again, Jesus is the perfect example. Jesus's ultimate power from within brought peace. Remember the time the disciples and Jesus were in the boat on the lake. A terrible storm came up, and the men were afraid for their lives. They woke Jesus, who was peacefully resting there, and begged him to do something.

It was obvious to Jesus, and can be to us Christians, that the disciples were afraid to the point of being completely void of peace from within, which in turn displayed its lack of presence from without. Jesus identified a major cause of this lack of peace when he made it known to the frightened group that they were men of little faith. Unless faith dwells inwardly, there will be no peace.

The peace of Jesus was displayed through power outwardly as he rebuked the storm and said from within, "Peace, be still." Everything was then calm. The wind diminished, the sea relaxed, and the hearts of the disciples were filled with peace. This is an obvious lesson to the Christian as we make our way through the world.

Another perfect example of our Savior is displayed through his recorded Word, as was evidenced the night he was to be arrested. "Peace I leave with you; my peace I give you. I do not give to you as the world gives. Do not let your hearts be troubled and do not be afraid" (John 14:27). It is the production of the fruit by Jesus and it being given to his disciples to bear (and for us to bear as well) that gives us the wonderful opportunity to bear the fruit of peace in life.

My recent experience with the heart dilemma brought occasion for me to learn the fruit of peace and also bear it for Jesus. It did take a great amount of faith for inward peace to truly be borne. From the moment of the initial attack to my sitting here today, Jesus's peace has been my choice, combined with confident faith that I believe the fruit of peace is being borne for the Lord. Not to drag the story out, I will give three instances concerning the heart-related journey.

Upon realizing I was having a heart attack, I immediately put myself in the hands of Jesus. When I told Elaine I felt my time was up, though I was concerned for her, I had peace. My peace was due to this state of calm, even though the pain in my body was gripping, which I drew from Jesus's peace, as I have advised other Christians to do. I had immediate calmness from within. The lessons I've learned as a Christian, whether through prayer, study, preaching, or hands-on daily reality, all came to light. I knew in my heart my Lord was in control, and Elaine and I both accepted fully the eventual outcome. Of course, we hoped and prayed for excellent resolve on this end of life, though we knew without a doubt that should I have faded into eternity, faith had gotten me there through having Jesus as my Savior and the Holy Spirit within my saved soul as Comforter, Counselor, and Guide. I was reminded then, as I am now, of the following scripture: "And the peace of God, which passeth all understanding, shall keep your hearts and minds through Christ Jesus" (Philippians 4:7 KJV).

After the trauma of the initial attack, when I was in a hospital bed awaiting surgery, I made a promise to the Lord. This was done out of peace. Recall my encouragement to you concerning confidence; this is an avenue from where I was reminded of inward peace. From the day of the attack the Lord carried on the peace I had within through my spirit. It was the Holy Spirit flowing through my soul who continually reminded me to be calm and cooperate, no matter how agitated I could become. I made the promise to the Lord I would remain calm, to the best of my ability, but I would place my trust and confidence in the Holy Spirit to see me through. It worked to a large degree.

I am now reminded of another heart-seated scripture subject I've preached on numbers of times and still know and believe the reality of. "Let the peace of Christ rule in your hearts, since as one body you were called to peace. And be thankful. Let the word of Christ dwell in you richly as you teach and admonish one another with all wisdom, and as you sing psalms, hymns and spiritual songs with gratitude in your hearts to God. And whatever you do, whether in word or deed, do it all in the name of the Lord Jesus, giving thanks to God the Father through him" (Colossians 3:15–17).

Lying in the hospital was unnerving enough. IV tubes leading into my body were not the most comfortable thing. And this was my condition *before* surgery. I continued to pray for the Holy Spirit's guidance and Jesus's peace. I believe the fruit was borne by way of being told through the nursing staff and the doctors that I was very cooperative and my demeanor was appreciated. They were recipients of the fruit produced through me by the Spirit and were consumers of the Spirit's fruit of peace borne by me in Jesus's name.

A third thing I am reminded of as a result of the heart event happened after my surgery. Surely I was in pain when I awoke from the operation. The first thing I recall is the feeling of drowning. I realized a breathing tube was in my throat. I tried to indicate to the medical attendants that I was drowning, I was assured I was okay and the tube would be coming out momentarily. This info didn't seem to help calm my fright. I can't tell you whether I spoke to the Lord at that moment, but I do know a calming peace came over me. Before I knew it, the tube was removed, and the drowning feeling immediately subsided. Peace permeated my soul. Tubes were going in every direction. IVs were more abundant than I remembered them being a day earlier. Tubes in my stomach and elsewhere were protruding. Cause for more panic was in order, but the peace of Christ covered me. Several days and many hours of recovery later, I was released from the hospital.

My journey on the road to recovery continued at home. Many trying hours of being uncomfortable and in pain lingered. It was the inward peace of the Lord that continued to make a huge difference. It wasn't just me receiving this awesome peace; Elaine was receiving the blessing as well. The fruit of peace was being produced within each of us as we continued to place our trust confidently in the Lord. The evidence was the inward fruit of peace shared between us.

I am pleased to report that nine weeks after surgery, I am up and around. I'm writing to you, my Christian friend, and I am celebrating, along with my beautiful wife, the fruit of the Holy Spirit in abundance—peace.

CHAPTER 16

Patience

Shifting from inward, the next three fruits of the Spirit, as Billy Graham suggests, point God-ward. Again, it isn't difficult to see through Christian eyes how feasible this idea really can be. Patience, kindness, and goodness—the three stand as a tripod. One leg faithfully stands with the others as the trio supports the soul with the agape love of God from within the redeemed soul and reciprocates to our Creator in the form of lasting fruit. This lasting fruit also is made available to those around us. We bear it while they receive it. The quality of the fruit remains ours to determine.

Patience is known as a virtue. It is indeed a gift—one that comes to many of us with a grain, or maybe a spoonful, of salt. Out of the nine fruits of the Spirit, I would vote the most difficult of the lot to bear faithfully is patience, with the possible exception of self-control. Let's focus on Patience. I believe that when we discuss the latter, a good foundation will have been set through the bearing of the other array of fruits.

Are you a patient Christian? Notice I didn't ask if you were a patient person. It is the blessing of Jesus that you are one of his. You are redeemed by his precious blood. There are many people in this world who can be considered patient. I've been in the company of lots of folks who display the quality and sometimes wonder if we Christians should take a closer look at the example-setter—Jesus.

Have you been around impatient Christians? Allow me to give you one of my observations—a clear example of a type of impatient Christian. I used to drive sixty miles one way to get to some of my jobs. The road I traveled was not very busy—definitely not like metro traffic. Making it a point to drive according to the speed limit, I was one of the few to adhere to the posted signage. On more than one occasion while cruising at the posted speed, I would see an approaching vehicle racing up from behind. I held my speed in patience. Unfortunately, the other driver found it necessary to push. With this becoming a frequent occurrence over time, I began to pray for the patience and peace of the pushy drivers. After the time spent waiting for another vehicle to pass me, I would eventually get an opportunity to view the rear end of the overtaking vehicle. Lo and behold, in many cases, the person now in front of me had, proudly displayed, a Christian fish symbol on the trunk lid. Needless to say, patience was a lacking virtue of that Christian—whether permanently or partially.

Have you ever prayed for patience? I advise you to know that God will be very pleased to answer the prayer. It may be wise to pray for the fruit of patience to be produced through you by the Spirit, with you being the bearer of the lasting fruit. Look back for a moment. Can you remember saying something like "Give me patience, Lord," and truly receiving ample opportunity to practice the gift, just to find yourself in more of a pickle than originally experienced? I'll admit I did so plenty of times till I came to the understanding of the Holy Spirit and his fruit from within. I'm still tempted to throw in the towel and plead to the Lord for the needed dose. I find it's better to let him produce the fruit that I can bear in Jesus's name, through Jesus's enduring example. By doing so, this brings honor to God and also blesses those around us.

I don't quite know if bearing patience applies to stubborn bolts on a vintage carburetor, but I know it supports the soul's feeling the frustration. Many people I've spoken to about patience will relate it to something like the stubborn-bolt theory, the frustrations of barking dogs, the unfound cause of a squeak inside a car, and so forth. Little annoyances become major issues with folks. This is where patience, or the lack thereof, begins to wear very thin. This is where we, as Christians, need to step up to the plate. It is through our declaring Jesus the Victor and the Holy Spirit the Guide that we exercise faith and begin to practice patience. Notice I used the word "practice." How about the old adage, "Practice makes perfect." This may apply through strenuous labor, and on the other hand, it may work nicely through fruit bearing. Strenuous labor is a good thing for the body, but does it necessarily need to be applied to the soul? I'll be careful here. Yes. We are to strain in prayer when the event arrives, just like the example of Jesus praying in the garden. Straining can and does bring needed patience.

I've discussed joy. No matter the style of practicing patience, the result can surely be realized through the blessing of Joy. Jesus was no stranger to desiring that his joy would be made complete. He faithfully displayed patience with the group who continually dogged him. The final straw of patience came to Jesus when he was brought to trial, unjustly, no fewer than six times in one night. Adding insult to injury only compounded that which could have worn Jesus's patience so thin he very honestly could have summoned a legion of angels to his rescue. The Lord didn't do this. Jesus bore the frustration and took it all to the cross. In his last minutes of life, Christ Jesus said, out of love, joy, peace, and patience—among the other fruits of the Spirit—"Father forgive them. For they know not what they do." (Luke 23:34). A beautiful example of God-ward borne fruit!

Volumes can be written concerning patience. I believe that you, Christian, have enough of an explanation before you that you can enter into conversation with Jesus, the true vine, while you abide in him and he abides in you, asking for his patience. You will know the truth. You will be guided into patience. And you will bear the lasting fruit of the Spirit while remembering the depth of your commitment: ankle deep, knee deep, waist deep, or completely over the head.

The first leg of the tripod will be strengthened and will lend equal support to the others. God-ward will your fruit, borne for Jesus, be a wonderful testimony of him as your Father and to the Son as your Redeemer and to the Holy Spirit as your fruit-producing Sustainer. Patience—yes!

CHAPTER 17

Kindness

"And God raised us up with Christ and seated us with him in the heavenly realms in Christ Jesus, in order that in the coming ages he might show the incomparable riches of his grace, expressed in his kindness to us in Christ Jesus" (Ephesians 2:6–7). This is the original kindness God displays and lovingly rests upon us. Isn't it wonderful that we have the opportunity to share this God-given kindness with those around us? By doing so, we have the second leg of the tripod already filled with strength and grace. This product of God's agape love is a stabilizer for each and every Christian—If we allow it to be. Let's look at the following verse of the above scripture to further be strengthened by the Lord that we may bear this lasting fruit of the Spirit—kindness. "For it is by grace you have been saved, through faith and this not from yourselves, it is a gift of God—not by works, so that no one can boast" (v. 8).

This is an excellent place to take a good look at the bearing of the fruit of the Spirit. To reiterate, kindness is one of the fruits we have the honor to bear for Jesus, as are all the fruits. Though we are following the suggestion of Billy Graham of the nine fruits and three thoughts of direction, or origin, it is very important to note, as I am sure Dr. Graham will agree, that *all* the lasting fruits borne by the Christian are to return to God—God-ward. If this were not the case, we would have no place in the kingdom of God, Jesus would not have come to this earth to pay our sin penalty, and therefore the Holy Spirit would not be our Guide, Counselor, and Comforter.

With this being said, and emphasizing God's kindness, let's read Ephesians 2:10: "For we are God's workmanship, created in Christ Jesus to do good works, which God prepared in advance for us to do."

At the beginning of this book, I stated the importance of God's agape love. And this pure love has woven itself through this work. I will repeat the scripture involving Jesus praying to the Father the night he was to be arrested. This very importantly ties to Ephesians 2:10. "Father, I want those you have given me to be with me where I am, and to see my glory, the glory you have given me because you loved me before the creation of the world" (John 17:24).

It is God's agape love—the love that loved Jesus before the creation of the world—that has overwhelmingly overflowed upon, within, and without us, the redeemed in Christ, that we have such a blessed opportunity to bear his fruit of kindness. What sort of representatives of Christ are we if we bear fruit other than true fruit from the true vine produced by the Holy Spirit, who guides us into all truth? Once again, let's be reminded of our personal walk with Jesus as we visit the fruit of the Spirit while allowing him to reveal his perfect example he is giving us to follow.

Scripture tells us that "we are God's workmanship, created in Christ Jesus." Christian, we are not created in anyone else other than Jesus, and more so, we are redeemed by his precious blood. Now that we are redeemed, we can do the work God has prepared in advance for us to do. Kindness is among the works. Notice we are also told in verse eight that we have been saved by grace, and that this grace is of God. It was he who created us in Christ Jesus—his Son—and the work of Jesus saved our souls. There was no work on our part. It was strictly the grace and kindness of God that reconciled us to him. It is this grace and kindness as demonstrated by Jesus that we are to display as his representatives. It is this fruit of the Spirit we cheerfully share with those around us. This form of lasting fruit of the Spirit will and does reciprocate God-ward to our Father.

Speaking of the fruit of kindness, have you borne any for the Lord today? There are myriad forms of kindness. You could spend the rest of your Christian life bearing this lasting fruit and never run out of places to bear it. Here's an important note: You are a fruit bearer. You are not a fruit producer. Take, for instance, the fruit at hand. Kindness has already been put in place as a result of the agape love of God. There is nothing more you can add to it. Your duty as a Christian is to follow the lead of the Holy Spirit and the command of Jesus, the true vine, and willingly allow the fruit of kindness and all the other fruits to be produced unhindered within your redeemed soul. It is through this divine process of the will of the Father that he created you in Christ Jesus to do good works, which he prepared in advance for you to do. God has already prepared. You and I are to carry out the plan by bearing the quality, lasting fruit—in this case, the fruit of the Spirit: kindness.

God's Word is an excellent place to explore the fruit of his kindness. It will strengthen your soul as you allow the Holy Spirit to guide you. Listen to what Jesus promised you and me out of his divine kindness. "And I will ask the Father, and he will give you another Counselor to be with you forever—the Spirit of truth … When the Counselor comes, whom I will send to you from the Father, the Spirit of truth who goes out from the Father, he will testify about me." (John 14:15–17; 15:26 NIV). That is unblemished love, and it proceeds exclusively from God.

We who are his redeemed are to testify about Jesus, as is found in verse 27 of John 15. "And you also must testify, for you have been with me from the beginning." It is through the fruit of the Spirit that we are to testify. Today you can demonstrate that witness of Jesus in your life through the guiding of the Spirit of truth honoring the will of the Father by exercising his love-drenched gift to you—the fruit of the Spirit—kindness. You will be filled with joy as it freely and freshly reciprocates to God—God-ward.

As we take our personal stroll with Jesus while enjoying the fruit of the Spirit through his excellent example, let's picture a beautiful instance of his heart of kindness: 'People were bringing little children to Jesus to have him touch them, but the disciples rebuked them. When Jesus saw this, he was indignant. He said to them, "Let the little children come to me, and do not hinder them, for the kingdom of God belongs to such as these. I tell you the truth, anyone who will not receive the kingdom of God like a little child will never enter it." And he took the children in his arms, put his hands on them and blessed them.' (Mark 10:13—16).

The second leg of the tripod is firmly in place. Let's see the tripod to completion as we faithfully consider and learn to demonstrate the lasting fruit of goodness.

CHAPTER 18

Goodness

The third leg of the tripod is powerfully and originally set in place by God. Integrity, righteousness, and honesty are all part of goodness. Do you see this visible quality coming from any source other than Jesus? Have you ever been assured by someone with the words "trust me"? The only one we can really trust is our God—namely, the Father, the Son, and the Holy Spirit. Talk about a strong and reliable tripod! The Trinity of God is the ultimate strengthening of our saved Christian existence. It's nice to be able to put trust in people who are honest and truthful, isn't it? It is quite another thing to know assuredly 100 percent of the time the accuracy of trust that comes from the Lord. And as a result of willing obedience,we as the branches firmly abiding in the true vine, who faithfully abides in us, the lasting fruit of goodness brings a sweet savor from God and is returned to him God-ward through his willing redeemed souls.

Over the years of being a minister, I have realized the only absolute truth is found in God. His Word is none other than the source of complete truth. And this includes all the waywardness found scattered among some biblical characters. All the recording of these people and the instances of incidents is undisputed truth. When God's Word says a person did something for his own selfish gain, it's the truth. When the Word tells us of the genuineness of his Son, that Jesus wept, it's true. The same holds true for the truth of being righteous. God is righteous. There is none other. Scripture tells us, "There is no one righteous, not even one" (Romans 3:9).

Where does this goodness leave us, the redeemed? Are we left in the lurch? Do we skip over this fruit of the Spirit and move on to the next? Not hardly. The fruits of the Spirit are attributes of God. His attributes are rock solid. He has given them to you and me that we will bear the fruit he produces. It was through the only Righteous one, Jesus, that our capability of bearing fruit came about. It was Jesus's goodness that bought our redemption. It was Jesus who, out of his goodness, gave us the Holy Spirit to cover our souls with the cleansing blood to make us righteous. The flesh we occupy will never be purely righteous. As long as we are temples of God, his righteousness dwells within our saved souls. It is his integrity and honesty through his Spirit, which is directly connected to our cleansed spirit, that influences our mind, emotion, and will to desire to do what is right. And this goodness faithfully reciprocates to him God-ward. Integrity, righteousness, and honesty are powerful. They are powerful to us Christians because it is through these definitive truths of goodness that we bear the lasting fruit.

Let's look at goodness. This fruit, as borne by the Christian through the guiding of the Holy Spirit, brings truth to the recipient. It in turn reciprocates God-ward. Just as there are myriad acts of kindness, so are there acts of goodness. Just like all the other fruits of the Spirit, it is God being the producer within the saved soul. It is we who bear this Jesus-inspired fruit for others to receive as his witness for others to enjoy.

I'd like to share with you the fruit of goodness I receive from my wife, Elaine, on a daily basis. Allow me to first thank God for our blessed marriage of twenty-five years. My Elaine is a sweetheart. What a wonderful gift she has been to me from the Lord! I could easily write a book of our togetherness in Jesus. Instead I will share with you her recent fruit of goodness enveloped in the agape love of the Father, Son, and Holy Spirit.

I sit in my office today with love for my wife on my heart. It isn't solely due to her almost undying care for me of late. Yes, she has been super in my recovery from the heart repair. For almost four weeks, I was confined to my recliner except for bathroom breaks and meal times. Every step of the way, Elaine has been my helper. Never a moment of frustration has she shown. She faithfully took my vitals and recorded them, made sure I took the right pills at the correct times, spent hours with me when I knew she needed to be doing other things, and the like. Her list of what seemed to be nonstop care was remarkable. Goodness is the fruit of the Spirit I have been the recipient of from the goodness produced within my Elaine by the Holy Spirit while beautifully reflecting upon the lasting examples of goodness displayed by Jesus. And this assuredly returns to the Father—God-ward.

Honesty best describes Elaine's lasting fruit of goodness. There have been no strained smiles or under-her-breath comments. She, without a doubt, extends the lasting fruit of goodness even today, and it joyfully reciprocates God-ward to the Lord. He has truly received this goodness through Elaine's heart and mine as we faithfully stand as one in him. Our thanks for Jesus's goodness displayed on the cross and beyond have overwhelmed our spirits. The Holy Spirit continues to produce the fruit. And in her instance, Elaine continues to bear the fruit of goodness, as she has since the first day I met her.

God-ward do the fruits of patience, kindness, and goodness flow back to the Father. Let us realize the agape love of the Father through the beautiful love of Jesus and the undying guidance of the sustaining Holy Spirit. The tripod stands firm and strong. The fruits of the true vine are God's own that the branches bear.

CHAPTER 19

Faithfulness

What better way to define faithfulness than seeing Jesus as our Savior? It was his faithfulness that brought us to the place where we could be reconciled with the Father. There is a psalm that speaks of the faithfulness of God and certainly applies to the Father, Son, and Holy Spirit: "I will sing of the Lord's great love forever; with my mouth I will make your faithfulness known through all generations. I will declare that your love stands forever, that you established your faithfulness in heaven itself" (Psalm 89:1–2).

The one who came to this earth to bring sinful man back into relationship with the Father can be seen as the one the psalmist echoed. Jesus, knowing the task at hand, faithfully gave up his heavenly splendor to make himself nothing, taking the very nature of a servant, being made in human likeness. It is the beautiful picture of this brand of faithfulness we Christians are to follow. The depth of love our Savior displayed goes far beyond the heavens, and we are recipients of it. How blessed we are to have opportunity to be in the company of the Spirit of Jesus as we further travel the path with him as he shows us, individually, the fruit of the Spirit.

This brand of the fruit of the Spirit is that which is borne outwardly. We've visited six fruits of the Spirit thus far. Three display the love of God as best being seen as generated inwardly. These are love, joy, and peace. The next three fruits display a God-ward sense.

Patience, kindness, and goodness borne by the Christian through the guidance of the Holy Spirit bring honor to God as we truly share them through Jesus's wonderfully lasting example with others.

Faithfulness, gentleness, and self-control show themselves to be outward. Jesus is our best example of the outwardness of these fruits. Concerning faithfulness—and as iterated by the psalmist, echoing Christ's love for the Father and the generations—Jesus's faithful service on this earth truly demonstrates perfect love. Though he was sinless, Jesus refused to cop an attitude. He had plenty of opportunity to do so through observing the lack of man's faith in God. If it could be possible for the sinless Christ, he also could have had the opportunity to lose his own faith by way of the ignorance and disobedience of the very ones who were charged with informing the Hebrews of his very existence. Because of human pride and their failure to follow through with their God-appointed duty, this being as bad as slapping God in the face, Jesus could have been tempted to throw in the towel.

Jesus faithfully committed to a mission. This was a sealed promise, and he would do all it required to carry it through. His faithfulness was outwardly evident. His shoulders did not slump as he energetically put one foot in front of the other, blazing the path to eternity. From childhood to adulthood, Jesus continued to grow in wisdom and stature. Even in the most trying moments of his time on Earth, the Lord Jesus faithfully carried through the command of the Father that you and I would have redemption and the Spirit of truth living within our saved souls eternally.

Only Jesus could follow through with this brand of faithfulness. It is apparent that we Christians could never come close to what Jesus accomplished in our stead with unswerving faithfulness. By the same token, the fruit of faithfulness being produced from within our saved souls is a fruit we must share in all situations. And by doing so, we outwardly display the love Jesus so desired that we would demonstrate each day of our lives.

In Jesus's presence as you presently walk with him along this path of fruit-bearing, are you committed to purposely bringing outward glory to him through your fruit of faithfulness? Are you excited to make evident your fruit of faithfulness paramount? The fruit of faithfulness you bear for Jesus as a reflection of his own redeemed soul will surely outwardly shine light on the Lord as well. How wonderful the blessing of this truth!

What does the fruit of faithfulness look like to you? We hear some people talk about random acts of kindness. As referred to in the light of faithfulness, can this fruit be random? Do you feel you could bear a random act of faithfulness and call it lasting fruit just to possibly indicate you fulfilled a duty? All the fruits of the Spirit should be borne and shared freely and faithfully. Faithfulness has endurance. Look at Jesus's faithfulness; it endures unto this very moment and beyond. It is his perfect example that, once again, sets the course for us to follow.

Consider your home. It was God who provided it. Faithfulness to the Provider's provision will display your fruit of faithfulness outwardly.

See once again Jesus's faithfulness within the promise he made the night he was arrested: "Do not let your hearts be troubled. Trust in God; trust also in me. In my father's house are many rooms; if it were not so, I would have told you. I am going there to prepare a place for you, I will come back and take you with me that you also will be where I am. You know the way to the place where I am going." (John 14: 1—4).

Imagine Jesus making such a promise of a beautiful residence he is personally preparing for you and me. He is faithful in this promise. He, through example, demonstrates to you and me how we should be good stewards. When we enter into heaven—this place Jesus has prepared for each of us, we can rest assured, will be just as he said it will because of his faithfulness. Are we willing to take heed from the excellent steward and through this heavenly example bear the fruit of faithfulness? Even in the earthly residence he has provided for our occupancy?

If Jesus can make ready and maintain our mansion in heaven, can we not, out of faithfulness, maintain our own here on earth?

Though this has been a brick and mortar example let's be reminded, too, that the fruit of the Spirit, faithfulness, plays a very important role in our outward spiritual fruit- bearing for Jesus as we are also stewards of our spirits and bodies—his temple. In being steward of his temple do you desire to know your Lord more personally to experience what it is to be faithful on the inside—your spirit and on the outside—your body? For best results, daily reading of your Bible puts you in spiritual communion with him. The Holy Spirit helps you visit Jesus. Through his guiding in the Word you will become more intimate with Jesus and his healthy example of life. Remember his word to you: If you abide in me, and I abide in you, you will bear much fruit. Apart from me, you can do nothing (my paraphrase).

Remember the scene where you were invited to view the vine and branches from the inside. If you are willing to allow the Holy Spirit— the lifeblood of the vine—to fully consume you that you will bear unrestricted fruit of sweet savor, this sets the perfect tone for the results you will experience through daily bible reading.

The fruit of the Spirit—faithfulness—is far reaching. The more you bear this fruit, the more you will be filled with the agape love of God. This surely stands true with all the fruits the Spirit produces within your saved soul while you abide in Jesus, *the true vine.*

Purposefully bear the fruit of faithfulness for Jesus. It was his committed faithfulness that made it possible for you to have residing within your redeemed soul the Holy Spirit—the producer of the fruit you are capable of bearing. It's outward. It's beautiful. It's lasting. Combined with the lasting fruit of faithfulness, gentleness plays a major role in the outward display of the Christian. Do you believe you can have one without the other? Let's find out.

CHAPTER 20

Gentleness

What is your first recollection of gentleness? Did it possibly come through loving hands? Does it stem back to your childhood? Gentleness is a wonderful experience—especially when we are on the receiving end. It's also a powerfully wonderful thing when we are on the giving end. Gentleness resolves harsh issues if ministered with truth. Yes, there are times when it seems all the gentleness in the world will not meet with success. Putting our complete trust in the Holy Spirit is that step in the right direction we need to take to faithfully bear the lasting fruit of gentleness. Through his guidance, we can call upon compassion. In many cases, compassion is an ingredient of gentleness, and the lasting fruit of Jesus's faithfulness combined with gentleness proves to be a sweet savor. Let's see him demonstrate the fruit bearing.

I'm quite often writing stories with Bible-based themes. This past year I decided to write a first-person account of the disciples. It's interesting to think about what took place in the presence of Jesus during his time on earth. One particular account I wrote had a reference to Jesus's visit to the region of Tyre and Sidon. The story was written as if it were seen through the eyes of Nathanael and spoken through his voice. Setting the stage, I will begin where Philip had found the to-be disciple of Jesus and announced Jesus of Nazareth.

I think Jesus saw me as an observer quick to answer but also one who thought things through. Philip, my good friend, was the first to tell me of the Master. He was so excited when he found me here! He blurted out with no uncertainty that they had found the one Moses had written about in the law and whom the prophets had prophesied. In his exuberance, Philip had a gleam about him I had never seen before.

With a smile, he announced that the person of interest was Jesus of Nazareth, the son of Joseph. He couldn't have been more emphatic even if he'd had a handful of exclamation points standing at the ready to confirm the positive find.

I, with my matter-of-factness, poured forth with slicing precision. "Nazareth!" I complained. "What good can come from that place?" Without being the least bit fazed by my disrespectful scathe, Philip pleasantly said in an inviting way, "Come and see."

Almost embarrassed, I reflect upon the days that followed my first encounter with Jesus of Nazareth. One very important thing I learned from the Master was not to prejudge. As a matter of fact, he warned us that if we judge others, we should be prepared to be judged in the same manner. I have been reminded of this statement numbers of times as we encountered many opportunities to stand in presumption of others. If there was anybody more qualified to set the perfect example of his advice, it was Jesus. Gentleness was, by all means, one of his wonderful attributes.

We seemed to constantly trip over our tongues, but Jesus would help us reel them back in to our wide-open mouths by faithfully and gently setting examples. I remember one time when we had gone up into the region of Tyre and Sidon. The Master needed rest, since he had been barraged by large crowds of people wanting to be in his presence. As we were gathered in a quiet place having good conversation, a woman—a despised Gentile, a Syrophoenician— interrupted us. She came begging Jesus to heal her daughter, whom she claimed was possessed by a demon. He gave her no reply, as if to purposely ignore the woman. In judgment of her due to her low status, we heartlessly prompted the Master to tell her to go away. She fell on her knees, begging him to heal her child. Jesus calmly responded by saying he had come to help the Jew, not the Gentile, and that it wasn't right to take the children's food from them and throw it to the dogs.

In that moment, we all silently applauded the idea that Jesus had put this despised Gentile in her place and that she would leave without hesitation. Instead of satisfying our agitated whim, she quickly responded by telling the Master it was true what he had said, but that even the puppies beneath the table are given scraps from the children. To our dismay, Jesus gently spoke to her, saying she had responded correctly and she could go home in peace because he had healed her beloved daughter and the demon had left her. I think from that time on, because of the pure gentleness of Jesus, the group of us were painfully cut to the heart and became deeply aware of the danger of judging.

Lack of compassion on our part sabotages the fruit of gentleness, thus undermining faithfulness. It is obvious what would have come about had Jesus ordered the woman out of their presence. The saving grace is that he was compassionate and gentle—and faithfully so. The account in the Gospels doesn't tell us Jesus was agitated, as the disciples were. He listened to the woman and gave just cause as to why he was here. She must have known in her heart from accounts she had obviously heard of Jesus's healings that he was surely filled with compassion and gentleness and would be faithful in healing her beloved daughter. This proved to be true. This is a magnificent example of the outward fruit of gentleness.

What opportunity have you had to convert your sour fruit of rejection into lasting sweet fruit by showing compassionate gentleness undergirded by faithfulness? This is an outward sign, indeed, to be learned from the Master and shared plainly with others. The fruit of the Spirit is pure and wholesome. It has to be. It comes from *the true vine.*

At your nearest opportunity to display gentleness, faithfully do so. It will demonstrate the agape love of God and will also bring glory to the Father, Son, and Holy Spirit. And your spirit will soar as if on the wings of eagles.

CHAPTER 21

Self-Control

I had an incident occur in which I surely lacked the fruit of self-control. It was a beautiful day. My wife and I were in the shop, working on a customer's order. Unfortunately, my belt sander bit the dust—pun intended. We decided to go to a power tool distributor to purchase a new model. When we had successfully done so, we returned to the shop to resume production.

Sanding the pieces of wood required finesse. The new sander and brand-new belt bit into one of the crucial pieces. I was short on time to begin with. The old sander going down added to the loss of production time. Now the new sander, instead of saving time, caused more loss than gain. Knowing the delivery was to be made the next day, I became further enraged as every second needed to complete the project on time passed. In an instant, with both hands clenching the new machine, I lifted it high above my head and hurled it downward, violently slamming it to the floor. Pieces flew everywhere.

The next thing I knew, my wife was walking out of the shop. After a few minutes, I realized she was walking down the street, away from our bay. I got in my truck and caught up to her. Before I could say a word, she said, "I won't live with a violent man." She continued to walk. Following along, I begged her not to leave. She told me she would stay but added that I would have to learn self-control.

Needless to say, the message was taken to heart, and I immediately changed my way. This was the first time I had become so frustrated that I acted in such a harsh manner. I knew I wasn't willing to give up the love of my life because of a lack of self-control.

I'm sure I'm not the only person—Christian—in the world who has had a moment of rage. I found out early on that a lack of self-control wasn't going to destroy our marriage or my life. I can honestly say I have not pulled a stunt like that since, and that was about twenty-five years ago. Praise Jesus for his fruit of the Spirit—self-control.

Self-control is a wonderful gift of the Spirit. Let's look at the positive side of this vital attribute. After all, the fruit we are to bear for Jesus through the guiding of the Holy Spirit should be pleasing and inviting to those around us as we have thus far briefly seen demonstrated through the former fruits of the array. As truly as faithfulness and gentleness prove a savory outwardly display, so does self-control bring glory to Jesus. Christian, you and I have great opportunity to represent our Savior through such a calming fruit as we live as his ambassadors in this troubled world.

It would be difficult to demonstrate the essence of self-control while using you, my brother or sister in Christ, as the subject. Instead I will continue to use myself. Much of this gift has been instituted to my own blessing as well as to others with whom I am in communication and company. Another positive result of my heart attack has resulted out of obedience and self-control.

Obedience has a great deal to do with self-control, as do faithfulness and gentleness. First, the one who deserves the obedience is the one who gave us life. It was out of obedience to the Father that Jesus practiced self-control. Especially while hanging on the cross, with grueling pain wrenching every nerve and sinew of his beaten, nail-pierced body, Jesus was in complete self-control. He had a mission to complete. Without the completion of the duty, where would we be? Thanks to the Lord Jesus for demonstrating self-control to us. We have no excuse to not practice it and bear the fruit of it—lasting fruit bringing outward awareness.

The results of demonstrating self-control in my current life don't come close to those of Jesus. (It is important that stories of obedience be conveyed in all instances. It just so happens my story fits the bill for the moment.) My self-control began with obeying the instructions the doctors gave me from the get-go. I could have acknowledged them by way of verbally agreeing. Truly, what good would that have done? A truthless nod would have been of no benefit, but more so it would prove detrimental to my future health.

Certain strict guidelines were laid out for me to faithfully follow. By doing so, I would gain and maintain good health. A requirement of self-control was at hand. Believe it or not, we human beings get hooked on food. I'm talking food embellished with salt, salt, salt. This one ingredient is responsible for major cardiac disease, among other goodies. If you had asked me the day I had my heart event if I were hooked on salt, I would have laughed. My answer would have been a direct no. To my amazement, I surely was hooked on the stuff. The first meal I ate, or attempted to eat, in the hospital was completely salt less. My first thought was *This is terrible! Where's the salt? Even just a touch.* My becoming obedient began here. *Self-control* was obviously on the horizon.

Not willing to voluntarily go through another heart event, I planted it in my mind, heart, and soul to adhere to the new regimen. It was truly tough for the first several weeks. One of the things that helped immensely was Elaine's willingness to share the fruit of self-control with me. All our meals are prepared the same. Salt is out of the picture. New doctor-approved spices have replaced salt. Yes, they took some getting used to. Now I can honestly say—and I speak for me and my wife—we do not miss the salt. It took obedience, which led to self-control.

I am happy to say that because of this one change in my lifestyle, I feel excellent and I've lost thirty unneeded pounds. I'm also filled with energy and am walking seven miles per day; talking about examples to imitate, Jesus briskly walked the roads each day so why can't I follow his lead. The fruit of self-control is one I gladly bear as an outward witness to our Lord and Savior as being guided by the Holy Spirit.

Self-control is the last of the fruits of the Spirit as specified by the Bible in the letter of Paul to the Galatians. This important fruit of the Spirit can and will make a major impact on your life as a Christian. Also, your outward example can very well influence others around you to follow suit. This has held true for me. Since I've learned to eat without salt, some of my friends are (at least as a result of experimentation) losing the salt shaker.

This last statement may not be an affirmation of the fruit of self-control, but as I pointed out earlier in this book, it is completely up to us as redeemed believers to follow the lead of the Holy Spirit in the name of Jesus, the true vine, by the will of the Father that we, the branches, will faithfully bear the good and lasting fruit produced by the Father, Son, and Holy Spirit.

In your specific case, Christian, you are responsible for faithfully following through as the Holy Spirit guides you into all truth. And the fruit of the Spirit is no exception. Look at it from this point of view: Your obedience to the Lord and your bearing his fruit will always result in a blessing—for yourself and for others around you. On top of that, it will please your Creator, Savior, and Sustainer. What a multifaceted gift within itself! Yes, it all began with love, and it eternally continues to his glory.

I hope the invitation I made to you to walk the path with Jesus as an individual, and privately so, has proven beneficial to your future fruit-bearing for him. It has helped me to understand more of the unity I am enjoying in the presence of the Father, the Son and the

Holy Spirit while being over-the-head consumed within the river of life and the agape love of God.

The Spirit of God, the lifeblood who produces the fruit, also actively lives within your redeemed soul with power. What kind of power? Let's check it out.

CHAPTER 22

Power

Power has about it excitement. It is through the power of the Holy Spirit you have the opportunity to exercise your freedom in Christ Jesus. It is through this same power you were created. And this power raised Jesus from the dead. You also are indwelled by this power through the Holy Spirit, who powerfully ushered into your saved soul the agape love of the Father, the forgiveness of Jesus, your Savior, and eternal life sustained by the Spirit of God—namely the Holy Spirit.

In conclusion of this portion of *Yes! It All Began with Love*, it is important that you briefly know the power and the purpose of the Holy Spirit residing within your redeemed soul.

You are undoubtedly saved by the blood of Jesus through the will of the Father and are sustained by the power of the Holy Spirit. How you demonstrate this power is of maximum importance. There are many benefits to this power. There are also many dangers. By dangers I mean misuses. Unfortunately, there are some Christians who believe the Holy Spirit is exclusive. Without going into discussion stemming from a negative vein, I would like you to know that the power residing within your saved soul is not exclusive to you alone. He is the eternal Holy Spirit with whom you have become familiar through this writing and will hopefully learn more about and come to know more personally through his guiding you into God's Word—the Bible. Very importantly you have visited the eternal promise of Jesus, who assured through truth that you and I and every redeemed soul are permanently indwelled by the Holy Spirit. He, the Holy Spirit, is the power of God the Father, God the Son, and God the Holy Spirit actively working within you right this very minute.

He does not randomly come and go. The moment you accepted Jesus as your Savior, the Father instantaneously placed his Holy Spirit in your saved soul. You are indwelled forever. This is a one-time happening. The Holy Spirit will continue to fill you but never will reenter to take up residence, just as Jesus will never go to the cross again. There is no need of a coming and going of the Holy Spirit. A thorough reading of John 14—16 will reveal to you this truth. The promise Jesus made the night before he went to the cross for our redemption came to fruition on the Day of Pentecost, as is found in Acts 1—2.

Permanently indwelled by the Holy Spirit, we each are used of him through his power. To give an example, I am a redeemed believer just like you. The Lord chose for me to preach the Word of God. It took many years for this to occur, as you know from my testimony. It is through the power of the Holy Spirit working through me that his Word is delivered because of my faith and obedience. There is no exclusivity involved. You, Christian, are just as blessed as I, in that we both have the same Holy Spirit indwelling our individual redeemed souls. His work in your life is personal, but he is just as personal to each and every Christian.

The Holy Spirit is God's power residing in your saved soul, through the sacrifice of Jesus on the cross; his resurrection from the dead; and his glorious ascension into heaven. It is through this act of Jesus that he secured, with complete joy, his gift to you of the Holy Spirit. You are eternally sealed by the Holy Spirit and you are a bearer of the fruit of the Spirit. What more wonderful blessing could we, as brothers and sisters in Christ, ask for or even imagine? This is joy-filled cause for us to obey Jesus's command to love one another.

By faith, believe God's Word as truth. Jesus promised the Holy Spirit would indwell each and every one of us, and he absolutely is doing so.

As I mentioned several times, the Bible is the perfect source for your learning of the Holy Spirit, as he will lead you through your studies. Jesus said and promised he—the Holy Spirit—will lead you into all truth. It is through faith and belief I have given my heart to the Lord—to follow God's call to me to convey to you his original reason of agape love for giving you his Holy Spirit. May you be continually blessed as you allow the Spirit of truth to guide you into all truth by his power, which is universally shared with each redeemed soul saved through the will of the Father by the unconditional sacrifice of Jesus Christ and the all-inclusive indwelling of the Holy Spirit within the entire family of the saved.

Christian, allow the Spirit's power to be of benefit to you as you bear the lasting fruit of the Spirit and share the love of the Lord Jesus with your family, friends, and God's redeemed; and also the lost. Because of your relationship with the Holy Spirit, you will be better equipped to do the good works God has prepared in advance for you to do in Christ Jesus.

Hear Jesus's divine words of promise: "And I will ask the Father, and he will give you another Counselor to be with you forever—the Spirit of truth" (John 14:16). Also be reminded of the following: "[Jesus said,] I am the vine; you are the branches. If a man remains in me and I in him, he will bear much fruit; apart from me you can do nothing … You did not choose me, but I chose you and appointed you to go bear fruit—fruit that will last" (John 15:5, 16).

Praise be to God the Father, God the Son, and God the Holy Spirit!

Continue on, Christian! Know the one who will guide you.

CHAPTER 23

Born to Continue

You have been born to continue. Jesus told Nicodemus that everyone who wants to see the kingdom of God must be born again. You essentially have been born again to continue. And this continuance is possible only through the power and presence of the Holy Spirit in your redeemed born-again soul.

This is extraordinarily exciting news! You no longer stand in the ranks of the lost. You are now among the saved in the Lord Jesus Christ. By this truth being firmly in place, you are a child of God, permanently indwelled by the Holy Spirit.

Jesus promised the Spirit of truth, as you have been made aware. He joyfully delivered the promise through his unconditional sacrifice on the cross and his glorious resurrection from the dead. His ascension into heaven to be seated at the right hand of the Father qualified you and every born-again believer to receive the Holy Spirit as Guide, Counselor, and Sustainer. This is the magnificent truth each of us actively lives with every moment of every day.

The apostle Paul was so excited about the working of the Holy Spirit in his life and the lives of Christians that he left us this exhortation: "May the God of hope fill you with all joy and peace as you trust in him, so that you may overflow with hope by the power of the Holy Spirit" (Romans 15:13).

Having embarked upon the journey of knowing the Holy Spirit in my life, I believe I feel the exuberance Paul felt. Many hours of exposure to the Word of God have undergirded my spirit as I have embraced the Holy Spirit. This is the same opportunity you have. As I have said, the Holy Spirit is not exclusive. He is in you and is excitedly working within you. Now that you have been made aware of him, formally introduce yourself to the Counselor. Speak to him with joy-filled confidence as you wade into the blessed water.

You may have been brought to the point of ankle-deep awareness of the Spirit by way of this introduction. Now is your opportunity to wholeheartedly accept Jesus's promise and proceed further into the blessed waters. Headlong submersion is the Spirit's desire for you.

By acknowledging the Spirit of the Lord in your redeemed life on a daily and moment-by-moment basis, he will swing wide open the divine floodgates, and you will be amazed at the agape love of the Father—the eternal love that encompassed the Son from before the creation—and his Holy Spirit will become more than a daily reality to you. He will become personally known by you as you embrace his presence eternally.

You, Christian, have been introduced to the Holy Spirit, and he is no longer a passing subject in the Word of God. He is God actively working in your born-again soul. With power, he functions as Jesus's promise and the Father's will.

The things that can be said of the Holy Spirit are too many to ever be expressed, though great joy and love can be your drive as he guides you into all truth.

Making your decision for Jesus and being born again immediately ushered the Holy Spirit into your saved soul. Now that you have new life with Jesus, it is your gift from him that you can immediately continue. As the Holy Spirit has joyfully opened wide the heavenly door to you, faithfully open wide your heart to him. Yes, you have assuredly been born to continue, because it all began with love.

May the God of hope fill you with all joy and peace as you trust in him, so that you may overflow with hope by the power of the Holy Spirit.

It's Been My Pleasure

Thank you for allowing me to share this great news with you. Quite a few years have passed since the Holy Spirit noticeably became aware to me in my Christian life. I am deeply grateful to the Lord Jesus for guiding me through the many years I basically ignored him as the Holy Spirit residing within my saved soul.

I hope and pray the Holy Spirit has been simply introduced to you. I also pray you will be further inspired and guided by the Holy Spirit to search the Bible so you will be able to confirm the truths of the Spirit of God.

Yes! It All Began with Love is my first completed work regarding a book written on the Holy Spirit. Because of his utmost importance in my life as a Christian, I hope you realize now his same role in your life.

The Holy Spirit would be pointless if Jesus had not promised him to every redeemed believer. It is pertinent that each of us exercises the Spirit's grace and truth and faithfully bear lasting fruit for Jesus. It is most assured that God the Father, through his agape love, has given opportunity to whosoever will believe. This truth in and of itself spells out that the Holy Spirit powerfully indwells each and every Christian.

I purposely did not go into detail about certain facts of the Holy Spirit. Your future Bible studies will reveal him to you as he guides you into all truth. One thing I would like for you to be ever aware of is that the Holy Spirit is a person, just the same as the Father and the Son are persons. They make up the Godhead—the Holy Trinity.

Let me also call your attention to the "him," "he," "his," and "himself" in this writing. Per today's grammatical standards, and I have respectfully observed this rule in this writing, it is not proper to capitalize these references to God. Nevertheless, I personally hold to the Victorian idea that these designations are reverent. According to my upbringing, I choose to honor my Lord with such designation— such as in "Jesus is my Lord and Savior because He has forgiven me of my sin."

As your relationship with the Father, Son, and Holy Spirit comes into focus, you may also desire to embrace him in this manner of recognition, even if in a personal way. This designation truly gives witness to his Personhood.

Frequent reading of the scriptures, combined with daily prayer communication with the Trinity, will bring you to that closer relationship with the Godhead. Thus, your love for him will take on new meaning—to the point of desiring to give him full honor and praise, even in the sense of grammatical address.

In addition to reading this book through, take time to use *YES! It All Began with Love* as a daily devotional through separate chapters. I also suggest a group study such as in a Sunday school class & etc. You will find many blessings while you follow the lead of the Holy Spirit as he excitedly indwells your saved soul and, along with you, celebrates the truth of God's love for you.

Included in **part 2** are fifty Holy Spirit power guide prayers I have written that will help you focus on the Father, Son, and Holy Spirit. Also, in **part 3** I've included, for your quick reference, all the scriptures I have been able to find that directly show reference to the Holy Spirit. I was amazed at how many acknowledgments of the Spirit of the Lord are found throughout the Old and New Testaments. What a wonderful experience this has been!

May the agape love of God the Father fill your soul by way of Jesus, our Savior, and the Holy Spirit, our Sustainer.

It has truly been my pleasure to share with you.

Part 2

Fifty Days of Holy Spirit Power Guide Prayers

*True prayer is prayer in the Spirit, that is, the prayer
the Spirit inspires and directs.*

— R. A. Torrey

The following fifty prayers were drawn from the truth of Holy Scripture. Take time for the next fifty days to allow God to speak to you as you pray in the power of the Holy Spirit, to whom you have now been formally introduced. He will guide you through these prayers, that you will become more familiar with the Father, Son, and Holy Spirit in your redeemed life.

Also, be reminded of the ultimate sacrifice Jesus paid for the forgiveness of your sins, that you would have the Holy Spirit eternally residing powerfully within your soul.

There is nothing like the reality of intimate communication with the Lord!

May you be abundantly blessed!

Day One

Father, you are God the Creator.
Jesus, you are God the Christ.
Holy Spirit, you are God the Counselor.
Father, you are the ever-living Spirit
in the likeness of Jesus Christ
going out from heaven
in the Holy Spirit
powerfully living in me. Amen.

Day Two

My hope is not in the empty ways
handed down by the forefathers
but with the precious blood of Christ,
the perfect sacrifice
empowered within my soul
by the Holy Spirit. Amen.

Day Three

Through Jesus I believe
in God, who raised him from the dead
by the Holy Spirit,
who is the mind and power of God
and whose image is seen
in the splendor
of Jesus Christ, our Lord. Amen.

Day Four

I trust in Jesus Christ,
the Son of God,
through whom I received
the promise of God,

my eternal salvation,
and who baptized me with the Holy Spirit,
whom he promised me
and gave me to be my Empowerer,
my Counselor, and my Guide.
Because of this eternal truth, I will never be put to shame. Amen.

Day Five

For I was like a sheep going astray,
but now I have returned
to the Shepherd and Overseer
of my soul
through the will of the Father,
through the ultimate sacrifice of
Jesus Christ the Son,
and by
the baptism and power of the Holy Spirit
continually living in me. Amen.

Day Six

Father, in my heart
I set apart Christ as Lord,
who through the Holy Spirit
prepares me with his power and wisdom
to give an answer to anyone who asks me
to give a reason for the hope I have.
Thank you for your will, my God and Father. Amen.

Day Seven

Jesus, through your being put to death
in the body
and being made alive by the Spirit,
I have died to sin

with you,
and I have been made alive
in my spirit
by the Holy Spirit,
who raised You from the dead
and who is forever alive
with power
in my redeemed soul. Amen.

Day Eight

Lord, my true desire
is to live not according to my
sinful body
but to the will of God,
who resides within my soul
that I may know the power of God
actively working in
and through me
to the glory of
the Father, the Son, and the Holy Spirit.
How awesome is this! Amen.

Day Nine

I believe in God's plan
that the end is near.
I submit to the Holy Spirit,
believing his power will keep my mind
melded and clear
with the mind of Christ,
whose mind is the Spirit of God.
Trusting in this eternal truth, I submit to be self-controlled,
so I can pray with power and confidence,
knowing that only he can communicate

my prayers to the Father
with groans that my words cannot express. Amen.

Day Ten

Lord, it is my desire
to serve others
through the power you provide within me—
namely, the Holy Spirit.
It is my true desire to speak
through the power
of the Holy Spirit
residing within my soul
as one speaking the very words of God
so that you may be praised
through Jesus Christ, His Son. Amen.

Day Eleven

Because the Spirit of glory rests on me
and
the power of the Spirit resides within my soul,
I am confident
when I am insulted
because of your name, Jesus;
I will be overjoyed while giving praise
to you, Lord of Glory—
my Redeemer, my Rock,
and
my Power. Amen.

Day Twelve

Jesus, in my suffering
according to God's will,
I submit myself to

the faithful Creator
through his eternal promise
through your blood, Jesus,
and through your power, Holy Spirit,
eternally residing within my saved soul,
while I continue to do good. Amen.

Day Thirteen

My Lord, my desire is to bring
honor and glory to
God the Father,
God the Son,
and
God the Holy Spirit
through this greeting spoken to
all Christians
by
the apostle Peter;
through the
power of the Holy Spirit within me,
I cheerfully say,
"Peace to all of you
Who are in Christ." Amen.

Day Fourteen

Lord Jesus, the life submitted
to the Spirit
is
life and peace.
I choose this! Amen.

Day Fifteen

Your divine power
resides eternally
in my redeemed soul
and is freely given to me
for life and godliness
by
the grace, goodness, and glory
of
you, Father,
you, Jesus,
and
you, Holy Spirit. Amen.

Day Sixteen

Holy Spirit,
continually search my heart and tune my ears
and set my eyes upon Jesus
so I won't be fast to speak out
and I will be even slower to get angry.
By really listening to God's Word
through your connecting me,
I will be able to better do what the divine Word says.
Amen.

Day Seventeen

It is through you, Holy Spirit,
constantly working in me,
that I can add to my faith
goodness, knowledge, self-control, perseverance,
godliness, brotherly kindness, and love.
By possessing these qualities
in increasing measure

I will be motivated to be
more effective and increasingly productive
in my knowledge of Jesus Christ,
my Lord and Savior. Amen.

Day Eighteen

Lord,
facing many trials without you
would be a terrible thing.
Father, with you as my Creator,
and Jesus, with you as my Savior,
and Holy Spirit, with you as my indwelling Guide,
I face my trials with pure joy,
as this is a gift from you. Amen.

Day Nineteen

You, Holy Spirit,
are the mind of God
always reminding me of where I am
in the Lord Jesus.
It is through your continual searching
of my heart
that I am divinely notified and corrected
to faithfully stay the course
with your
Holy Spirit power. Amen.

Day Twenty

As the prophets of old were carried along
by you, Holy Spirit,
I know I am indwelled and endued
with your eternal power to understand
that the Lord Jesus Christ

came to this earth to shine and overcome
the darkness of sin
that I would have opportunity
to accept his forgiveness of my sins
and receive him as Lord and Savior.
You, Holy Spirit, permanently reside
in my redeemed soul.
Thank you, Father, Son, and Holy Spirit. Amen.

Day Twenty-One

Jesus, I am so confident
in the power of your resurrection
and
the promise of you, eternal Father,
that you are God the Creator;
Jesus, you are God the Christ; and
Holy Spirit, you are God the Counselor.
Father, you are the ever-living Spirit
in the likeness of Jesus Christ
going out from heaven
in the Holy Spirit
powerfully living in me. Amen.

Day Twenty-Two

You, Father,
you, Jesus,
and
you, Holy Spirit
in my saved soul
excitedly fill me with confidence!
I, as a child of God,
proclaim the
good news
of the coming of the kingdom.

I hear in my heart the very words of God:
"The Spirit and the bride say, 'Come!'
And let him who hears say, 'Come!'
Whoever is thirsty,
let him come;
and whoever wishes,
let him take the free gift
of the water of life."
And praise God! Christ is that free Gift of the Water of Life
and you, Holy Spirit, are his
Power working in all of us,
the Lord's children.
To God be the glory! Amen.

Day Twenty-Three

I put my trust in you, Lord.
You are my God.
You indwell my heart with your ever-living Spirit.
It is through your precious blood,
Jesus, my Savior, that has made it so.
In you, Father, Jesus, and Holy Spirit,
I firmly place my faith.
Amen.

Day Twenty-Four

Jesus,
It is through your eyewitnesses
that I am made more excited
about you—the Word of Life.
Your proclaiming of eternal life
enlivens my heart.
I undoubtedly know it was through the
Father's agape love and grace
and through your unselfish work on the cross

that I am redeemed,
and
as a magnificent result,
you, Holy Spirit, live in my soul.
And this makes my joy complete! Amen.

Day Twenty-Five

Holy Spirit,
thank you for reminding me that God is Light.
And if I walk in the Light,
I have fellowship with my brothers and sisters in Christ;
and his precious blood purifies us from all sin. Amen.

Day Twenty-Six

I am amazed
at your power, Holy Spirit, which
you, Father, and you, Jesus, have put within my redeemed soul.
And I am thankful to you, Holy Spirit,
for constantly reminding me of my weak flesh
that opens me up to sin.
Lord, thank you for giving me your Holy Spirit
to remind me that when I confess my sins,
you are faithful and just
and will forgive me of my sins
and will purify me from all unrighteousness. Amen.

Day Twenty-Seven

Jesus, I am grateful
to know you love me so much
that you want me to do your will.
I'm thankful that through your death and resurrection,
your promised Holy Spirit actively lives in me.

This is my assurance through his power within me:
I can do your will, and I live in you eternally. Amen.

Day Twenty-Eight

Lord, your eternal Word tells me I know the truth
because you have eternally anointed me and
all my redeemed brothers and sisters
with the Holy One—the Holy Spirit.
It is because of your universal anointing, Holy Spirit,
in all redeemed souls, that we know
the risen Son of God.
Through the Truth living within my soul—
namely you, Holy Spirit,
I firmly acknowledge
the Farther, the Son, and the Holy Spirit.
Amen.

Day Twenty-Nine

Through the confidence you have placed in my heart
since you redeemed me
with your precious blood,
I remain in you, Lord Jesus, and in the Father.
The promise you made to me and every believer is that we have
eternal life,
and this is guaranteed
by
you, Holy Spirit. Amen.

Day Thirty

Holy Spirit,
your anointing is on every Christian,
and
we receive it from you who remains in us.

Your anointing teaches me and all my
brothers and sisters in Christ
about all things
and
that your anointing is real.
Your anointing is not counterfeit.
Holy Spirit,
I willingly remain in you as you eternally remain in me. Amen.

Day Thirty-One

By your mighty power, Holy Spirit,
I trust in you for my continuance in Jesus,
so when he appears
I may be confident and unashamed
before Christ at his coming.
To the glory of the Father. Amen.

Day Thirty-Two

Father, your love is so great!
It's so great you have lavished
on me and my brothers and sisters in Christ
your eternal love!
And
you have made us your children!
We are your children, indwelled by
the Holy Spirit you promised through Jesus.
And when he appears, we will be like him.
How awesome is this, Lord!
Having this hope,
we are guided by your power, Holy Spirit,
to purify ourselves,
just as Jesus is pure.
We can do this only as you guide us into all truth, Holy Spirit,

as you faithfully convict and counsel us.
Thank you, Lord God! Amen.

Day Thirty-Three

Lord, I know I'm born of God.
I know that Jesus's precious blood covers my soul.
I know you, Holy Spirit, are powerfully working
in me to restrain me from sinning.
Though I am still in this body of flesh,
and it is prone to sin,
I trust in you, Holy Spirit,
to constantly keep me aware of sin lingering in my path.
I know because of your indwelling my redeemed soul
that God's seed remains in me,
and I'm reminded I must, by your indwelling power, put away sin.
Thank you, Holy Spirit, for your faithfulness! Amen.

Day Thirty-Four

You, Holy Spirit, reside in my redeemed soul.
You are greater than my heart,
and you know everything. Amen.

Day Thirty-Five

The Spirit of the Lord living in me
guides me into all truth.
It is my desire to continue to walk in the truth,
because there is no replacement for this.
Walking in the truth is walking in the light of Christ.
And doing so—walking in the truth and the
light of Christ—is doing what is good;
this truly is from God.
Thank you, Father, Son, and Holy Spirit.
Amen.

Day Thirty-Six

It's an awesome thing to recognize the Spirit of God!
According to your Word, Lord, there are acknowledging spirits
and denying spirits.
The denying spirits of men are dangerous, as are demon spirits.
You warn me and every Christian to be on guard against such.
They are not of you; they are of the antichrist.
Thank you for turning my spirit—my soul—to you
to gain your instruction and discernment.
Your Word tells us that every spirit acknowledging
that Jesus came in the flesh is from God.
And on the other hand,
every spirit that does not acknowledge Jesus is not from God.
Thank you, Father, for saving my spirit to
know Jesus as my Lord and Savior,
and to know the Holy Spirit, who indwells
my redeemed soul. Amen.

Day Thirty-Seven

Thank you, Holy Spirit, for residing
powerfully in my redeemed soul.
By your presence, I and my brothers and sisters in Christ
are overcoming the false spirits
because we are from God!
And you, being powerfully in me,
are
greater than the one who is in the world! Amen.

Day Thirty-Eight

Lord, your Word commands
that I believe in the name of your Son, Jesus Christ,
and that we love one another.
I am told that by obeying you,

I live in you and you in me.
And I know that you live in me,
because I know the Spirit you gave to me and to
each and every one of my brothers and sisters in Christ.
I am so grateful to you, Father, Son, and Holy Spirit! Amen.

Day Thirty-Nine

Wow!
You chose to give me new birth, Lord.
and through your Word of Truth,
I am like a type of firstfruit
of the entirety of all you've created!
This is awesome, Lord!
your good and perfect gifts
are from above,
and of these,
the gift of the Holy Spirit
is yours to me and
my brothers and sisters in Christ
through the unselfish sacrifice of Jesus.
And we are newly born in you!
Thank you for your love,
Father, Son, and Holy Spirit.
Amen.

Day Forty

Holy Spirit,
while I'm looking into God's Word
with your eternal wisdom guiding me,
it's like seeing myself in a mirror.
I see the true me and better understand
where correction is needed
and where the decency about me

can be an uplifting example to others.
Thank you. Amen.

Day Forty-One

Holy Spirit,
your opening of my mind is unfathomable.
You display God's love within me,
but I don't completely understand.
This is excellent cause for me,
your redeemed child,
to be dependent upon you.
Your Word tells me that I live in love
and live in God,
and he lives in me.
This makes my love complete.
Because of this,
God, who is love,
through your power within me,
the Holy Spirit,
equips me to be like him in this world.
Amen.

Day Forty-Two

Jesus,
your love is measureless!
Your divine Word assures me and my
brothers and sisters in Christ
that while we were yet sinners, you died for us;
and it was out of the Father's love
that you did this.
All inclusively, you sent the Holy Spirit
to take up divine residence
in our redeemed souls.
Through your perfect love residing in our souls,

you, Holy Spirit,
drive out fear! Amen.

Day Forty-Three

Because you loved us first, Lord,
we love.
Thank you for your unending love and patience in my soul.
Though things get tough in life
and our brothers and sisters test love and patience,
your perfect love,
powered up in my redeemed soul,
breaks down the walls of
anger, misunderstanding, rage, and
disappointment I sometimes feel
against my brother or sister in Christ.
Because of the Holy Spirit's presence within me,
your love shines forth to overcome adversity.
For this I thank you, Lord!
Because your command says that
if I love God,
I must love my brother and sister also.
Without your perfect love and power within me,
Holy Spirit,
this would be impossible.
With God, all things are possible! Amen.

Day Forty-Four

I am born of you, God,
because
I believe that Jesus is the Christ.
I also believe that everyone who loves you, Father,
loves your child as well.
My brothers and sisters in Christ are God's children.
It is your love in my redeemed soul

by the power of the Holy Spirit that guides me
to obey your commands.
Because of you, Spirit of God, residing within me,
God's commands are not burdensome.
I and my brothers and sisters in Christ
have overcome the world
because our faith has connected with you, Holy Spirit.
And through your guiding truth,
I believe in you, Jesus Christ, who overcame the world first.
Amen.

Day Forty-Five

I have eternal life
because of your sacrifice, Jesus—
the ultimate sacrifice you made for my sins
and the sins of all who believe.
Lord Jesus, because you came by water and blood,
I have,
through the water, been buried with you and raised up anew.
Through your precious blood shed on the cross,
I am eternally covered over and redeemed.
Through you, Holy Spirit, I have eternal life in Jesus
because
You, Father, you, Jesus, and you, Holy Spirit, agree as one
as you bear record in heaven.
The Spirit of truth—you, Holy Spirit—testifies in my redeemed soul
and the souls of all believers in Christ.
You, Holy Spirit, are the Spirit of truth residing in power
within my soul and in the soul of each
and every redeemed of Christ.
Amen.

Day Forty-Six

Father, though I hear the testimony of
others that Jesus is the Savior
and he sent the Holy Spirit to reside in my redeemed soul,
I rely on your testimony about Jesus first.
The best part is that anyone who believes in Jesus,
the Son of God,
has your testimony in his or her soul.
The Testimony in our souls is this:
Our eternal life is given to us by the Father,
and this eternal life is in Jesus,
and because of this, we who believe
have life.
This life is eternal.
Thank you, Jesus, for sending the Holy Spirit
into our redeemed souls in power
to seal us and to be our Guarantee of eternal life with you! Amen.

Day Forty-Seven

Father, Son, and Holy Spirit,
you work as one.
This truth is not totally understandable,
but by faith I believe.
Father, I know you promised redemption
of my once condemned soul.
You sent Jesus as your perfect sacrifice.
Through Jesus, you promised the Holy Spirit
to be my Counselor and Guide with power.
I believe all these divine things could happen only
through you, Father,
through you, Jesus,
and
through you, Holy Spirit;
and that you, as the one true God,

have lovingly redeemed and sealed my soul
and the soul of every believer.
Thank you, Lord!
Amen.

Day Forty-Eight

Dear Lord,
your apostle John wrote your words of encouragement
to the chosen lady and her children
two thousand years ago.
He did this in all truth.
His assurance was that she and her children knew the truth
—because of the Truth—
and your mighty Word tells us all:
"He lives with us all
and lives in us all,
even today!"
Praise you, Father, Son, and Holy Spirit,
for your Peace, Love, and Power
truthfully working within our redeemed souls.
Amen.

Day Forty-Nine

Lord,
you call my attention not to a new command
but to one that has been in front of
me and my brothers and sisters in Christ
since the beginning.
You tell us to walk in love
and to love one another.
Holy Spirit,
help me to daily walk
in this eternal love

as I obey the Father's command.
Amen.

Day Fifty

You, Spirit of the Lord living in me,
guide me into all truth.
It is my desire to continue to walk in the truth,
because there is no replacement for this.
Walking in the truth is walking in the light of Christ.
And doing so—walking in the truth and the
light of Christ—is doing what is good;
This truly is from God.
Thank you, Holy Spirit, for counseling, guiding, and correcting me
each day of my redeemed life and into eternity. Amen.

Part 3

Old Testament and New Testament Scriptures Concerning the Holy Spirit

Through my years of study, I have personally searched the Holy Bible for direct Holy Spirit–related text. The journey has been long, arduous, and revealingly exciting. I would like to encourage your extended study of the Holy Spirit by sharing with you the priceless treasures found in the following scripture verses. A cursory reading of the passages will set the stage for *your* lifelong journey and continued relationship with the Holy Spirit. I pray that these scriptures will assist you in your studies and that *Yes! It All Began with Love* will become a valuable asset to your library.

To have a more solid foundation of scripture knowledge is important. Diligent study, searching, and comparison of the scriptures will prove beneficial to you, Christian, through the enlightening and guiding of the Holy Spirit. At the Creation and during the early centuries, the Holy Spirit was present and working. Equally so was he active in Jesus's incarnation, birth, ministry, death, and resurrection, such as is found before Pentecost. His present work has increased in the church since the great day of his universal indwelling of the redeemed. Inclusive with, above, and throughout this age of grace, all of which link perfectly with the prophesied future events that will come to pass into and beyond the time of the Revelation at the Second Coming of Jesus, God's Word unmistakably reveals the Holy Spirit in all truth.

The Holy Spirit—which Jesus promised you and me—is your willing guide. Prayerfully allow him to inspire and enlighten your saved soul as your spirit melds with him. May you be abundantly blessed as you follow him while he leads you through the scriptures, guiding you into all truth.

Old Testament Scriptures
Concerning the Holy Spirit

Genesis 1:2: Now the earth was formless and empty, darkness was over the surface of the deep, and the Spirit of God was hovering over the waters.

Genesis 6:1–3: When human beings began to increase in number on the earth and daughters were born to them, the sons of God saw that the daughters of humans were beautiful, and they married any of them they chose. Then the LORD said, "My Spirit will not contend with humans forever, for they are mortal; their days will be a hundred and twenty years."

Exodus 31:1–5: Then the LORD said to Moses, "See, I have chosen Bezalel son of Uri, the son of Hur, of the tribe of Judah, and I have filled him with the Spirit of God, with wisdom, with understanding, with knowledge and with all kinds of skills— to make artistic designs for work in gold, silver and bronze, to cut and set stones, to work in wood, and to engage in all kinds of crafts."

Exodus 35:30–33: Then Moses said to the Israelites, "See, the LORD has chosen Bezalel son of Uri, the son of Hur, of the tribe of Judah, and he has filled him with the Spirit of God, with wisdom, with understanding, with knowledge and with all kinds of skills— to make artistic designs for work in gold, silver and bronze, to cut and set stones, to work in wood and to engage in all kinds of artistic crafts."

Numbers 11:16–17: The LORD said to Moses: "Bring me seventy of Israel's elders who are known to you as leaders and officials among the people. Have them come to the tent of meeting, that they may stand there with you. I will come down and speak with you there, and I will take some of the power of the Spirit that is on you and put it on them. They will share the burden of the people with you so that you will not have to carry it alone."

Numbers 11:24–30: So Moses went out and told the people what the LORD had said. He brought together seventy of their elders and had them stand around the tent. Then the LORD came down in the cloud and spoke with him, and he took some of the power of the Spirit that was on him and put it on the seventy elders. When the Spirit rested on them, they prophesied—but did not do so again. However, two men, whose names were Eldad and Medad, had remained in the camp. They were listed among the elders, but did not go out to the tent. Yet the Spirit also rested on them, and they prophesied in the camp. A young man ran and told Moses, "Eldad and Medad are prophesying in the camp." Joshua son of Nun, who had been Moses' aide since youth, spoke up and said, "Moses, my lord, stop them!" But Moses replied, "Are you jealous for my sake? I wish that all the LORD's people were prophets and that the LORD would put his Spirit on them!" Then Moses and the elders of Israel returned to the camp.

Numbers 24:1–9: Now when Balaam saw that it pleased the LORD to bless Israel, he did not resort to divination as at other times, but turned his face toward the wilderness. When Balaam looked out and saw Israel encamped tribe by tribe, the Spirit of God came on him and he spoke his message: "The prophecy of Balaam son of Beor, the prophecy of one whose eye sees clearly, the prophecy of one who hears the words of God, who sees a vision from the Almighty, who falls prostrate, and whose eyes are opened: How beautiful are your tents, Jacob, your dwelling places, Israel! Like valleys they spread out, like gardens beside a river, like aloes planted by the LORD, like cedars beside the waters. Water will flow from their buckets; their seed will have abundant water. Their king will be greater than Agag; their kingdom will be exalted. God brought them out of Egypt; they have the strength of a wild ox. They devour hostile nations and break their bones in pieces; with their arrows they pierce them. Like a lion they crouch and lie down, like a lioness—who dares to rouse them? May those who bless you be blessed and those who curse you be cursed!"

Judges 3:9–10: But when they cried out to the Lord, he raised up for them a deliverer, Othniel son of Kenaz, Caleb's younger brother, who saved them. The Spirit of the Lord came on him, so that he became Israel's judge and went to war.

Judges 6:34: Then the Spirit of the Lord came on Gideon, and he blew the trumpet, summoning the Abiezrites to follow him.

Judges 11:29–30: Then the Spirit of the Lord came on Jephthah. He crossed Gilead and Manasseh, passed through Mizpah of Gilead, and from there he advanced against the Ammonites. And Jephthah made a vow to the Lord: "If you give the Ammonites into my hands, whatever comes out of the door of my house to meet me when I return in triumph from the Ammonites will be the Lord's, and I will sacrifice it as a burnt offering."

Judges 13:24–25: The woman gave birth to a boy and named him Samson. He grew and the Lord blessed him, and the Spirit of the Lord began to stir him while he was in Mahaneh Dan, between Zorah and Eshtaol.

Judges 14:5–7: Samson went down to Timnah together with his father and mother. As they approached the vineyards of Timnah, suddenly a young lion came roaring toward him. The Spirit of the Lord came powerfully upon him so that he tore the lion apart with his bare hands as he might have torn a young goat. But he told neither his father nor his mother what he had done. Then he went down and talked with the woman, and he liked her.

Judges 14:19–20: Then the Spirit of the Lord came powerfully upon him. He went down to Ashkelon, struck down thirty of their men, stripped them of everything and gave their clothes to those who had explained the riddle. Burning with anger, he returned to his father's home. And Samson's wife was given to one of his companions who had attended him at the feast.

Judges 15:14–15: As he approached Lehi, the Philistines came toward him shouting. The Spirit of the Lord came powerfully upon him. The ropes on his arms became like charred flax, and the bindings dropped from his hands. Finding a fresh jawbone of a donkey, he grabbed it and struck down a thousand men.

1 Samuel 10:9–10: As Saul turned to leave Samuel, God changed Saul's heart, and all these signs were fulfilled that day. When he and his servant arrived at Gibeah, a procession of prophets met him; the Spirit of God came powerfully upon him, and he joined in their prophesying.

1 Samuel 11:6: When Saul heard their words, the Spirit of God came powerfully upon him, and he burned with anger.

1 Samuel 16:13: So Samuel took the horn of oil and anointed him in the presence of his brothers, and from that day on the Spirit of the LORD came powerfully upon David. Samuel then went to Ramah.

1 Samuel 16:14: Now the Spirit of the LORD had departed from Saul, and an evil spirit from the LORD tormented him.

1 Samuel 19:19–23: Word came to Saul: "David is in Naioth at Ramah"; so he sent men to capture him. But when they saw a group of prophets prophesying, with Samuel standing there as their leader, the Spirit of God came on Saul's men, and they also prophesied. Saul was told about it, and he sent more men, and they prophesied too. Saul sent men a third time, and they also prophesied. Finally, he himself left for Ramah and went to the great cistern at Seku.

And he asked, "Where are Samuel and David?" "Over in Naioth at Ramah," they said. So Saul went to Naioth at Ramah. But the Spirit of God came even on him, and he walked along prophesying until he came to Naioth.

2 Chronicles 15:1–7: The Spirit of God came on Azariah son of Oded. He went out to meet Asa and said to him, "Listen to me, Asa and all Judah and Benjamin. The LORD is with you when you are with him. If you seek him, he will be found by you, but if you forsake him, he will forsake you. For a long time Israel was without the true God, without a priest to teach and without the law. But in their distress they turned to the LORD, the God of Israel, and sought him, and he was found by them. In those days it was not safe to travel about, for all the inhabitants of the lands were in great turmoil. One nation was being crushed by another and one city by another, because God was troubling them with every kind of distress. But as for you, be strong and do not give up, for your work will be rewarded."

Nehemiah 9:19–20: Because of your great compassion you did not abandon them in the wilderness. By day the pillar of cloud did not fail to guide them on their path, nor the pillar of fire by night to shine on the way they were to take. You gave your good Spirit to instruct them. You did not withhold your manna from their mouths, and you gave them water for their thirst.

Nehemiah 9:29–31: You warned them in order to turn them back to your law, but they became arrogant and disobeyed your commands. They sinned against your ordinances, of which you said, "The person who obeys them will live by them." Stubbornly they turned their backs on you, became stiff-necked and refused to listen. For many years you were patient with them. By your Spirit you warned them through your prophets. Yet they paid no attention, so you gave them into the hands of the neighboring peoples. But in your great mercy you did not put an end to them or abandon them, for you are a gracious and merciful God.

Job 26:13: By his breath the skies became fair; his hand pierced the gliding serpent. [Note: According to the original Greek, "breath" connotes God's Spirit.]

Job 27:1–5: And Job continued his discourse: "As surely as God lives, who has denied me justice, the Almighty, who has made my life bitter, as long as I have life within me, the breath of God in my nostrils, my lips will not say anything wicked, and my tongue will not utter lies. I will never admit you are in the right; till I die, I will not deny my integrity." [See note on Job 26:13.]

Job 33:4 The Spirit of God has made me; the breath of the Almighty gives me life.

Job 34:12–15: It is unthinkable that God would do wrong, that the Almighty would pervert justice. Who appointed him over the earth? Who put him in charge of the whole world? If it were his intention and he withdrew his spirit and breath, all humanity would perish together and mankind would return to the dust.

Psalm 51:10–12: Create in me a pure heart, O God, and renew a steadfast spirit within me. Do not cast me from your presence or take your Holy Spirit from me. Restore to me the joy of your salvation and grant me a willing spirit, to sustain me. [Note: This is a case where the Holy Spirit was indwelling King David, and he feared God would remove the Spirit from him. This was possible at that time, as the Holy Spirit had not yet been announced as universal to all believers. The universal indwelling magnificently would and did occur on the Day of Pentecost. Jesus's promise to the "whosoever" would believe was made permanent that day.]

Psalm 104:27–32: All creatures look to you to give them their food at the proper time. When you give it to them, they gather it up; when you open your hand, they are satisfied with good things. When you hide your face, they are terrified; when you take away their breath, they die and return to the dust. When you send your Spirit, they are created, and you renew the face of the ground. May the glory of the Lord endure forever; may the Lord rejoice in his works—he who looks at the earth, and it trembles, who touches the mountains, and they smoke.

Psalm 106:32–33: By the waters of Meribah they angered the LORD, and trouble came to Moses because of them; for they rebelled against the Spirit of God, and rash words came from Moses' lips.

Psalm 139:7: Where can I go from your Spirit? Where can I flee from your presence?

Psalm 143:10: Teach me to do your will, for you are my God; may your good Spirit lead me on level ground.

Isaiah 6:9–10: He said, "Go and tell this people: 'be ever hearing, but never understanding; be ever seeing, but never perceiving.' Make the heart of this people calloused; make their ears dull and close their eyes. Otherwise they might see with their eyes, hear with their ears, understand with their hearts, and turn and be healed." [Note: This same scripture is found in Acts 28:26–27, preceded in verse 25 by the apostle Paul with the statement "The Holy Spirit spoke the truth to your ancestors when he said through Isaiah the prophet ..." Notice that "he" and "the Holy Spirit" are one and the same.]

Isaiah 11:2: The Spirit of the Lord will rest on him—the Spirit of wisdom and of understanding, the Spirit of counsel and of might, the Spirit of knowledge and fear of the Lord—

Isaiah 32:14–20: The fortress will be abandoned, the noisy city deserted; citadel and watchtower will become a wasteland forever, the delight of donkeys, a pasture for flocks, till the Spirit is poured on us from on high, and the desert becomes a fertile field, and the fertile field seems like a forest. The LORD's justice will dwell in the desert, his righteousness live in the fertile field. The fruit of that righteousness will be peace; its effect will be quietness and confidence forever. My people will live in peaceful dwelling places, in secure homes, in undisturbed places of rest. Though hail flattens the forest and the city is leveled completely, how blessed you will be, sowing your seed by every stream, and letting your cattle and donkeys range free.

Isaiah 42:1: Here is my servant, whom I uphold, my chosen one in whom I delight; I will put my Spirit on him, and he will bring justice to the nations.

Isaiah 44:1–5: But now listen, Jacob, my servant Israel, whom I have chosen. This is what the LORD says— he who made you, who formed you in the womb, and who will help you: Do not be afraid, Jacob, my servant, Jeshurun, whom I have chosen. For I will pour water on the thirsty land, and streams on the dry ground; I will pour out my Spirit on your offspring, and my blessing on your descendants. They will spring up like grass in a meadow, like poplar trees by flowing streams. Some will say, "I belong to the LORD"; others will call themselves by the name of Jacob; still others will write on their hand, "The LORD's," and will take the name Israel.

Isaiah 48:16–22: "Come near me and listen to this: From the first announcement I have not spoken in secret; at the time it happens, I am there." And now the Sovereign Lord has sent me, endowed with his Spirit. This is what the Lord says—your Redeemer, the Holy One of Israel: "I am the Lord your God, who teaches you what is best for you, who directs you in the way you should go. If only you had paid attention to my commands, your peace would have been like a river, your well-being like the waves of the sea. Your descendants would have been like the sand, your children like its numberless grains; their name would never be blotted out nor destroyed from before me." Leave Babylon, flee from the Babylonians! Announce this with shouts of joy and proclaim it. Send it out to the ends of the earth; say, "The LORD has redeemed his servant Jacob." They did not thirst when he led them through the deserts; he made water flow for them from the rock; he split the rock and water gushed out. "There is no peace," says the LORD, "for the wicked."

Isaiah 59:19–21: From the west, people will fear the name of the LORD, and from the rising of the sun, they will revere his glory. For he will come like a pent-up flood that the breath of the LORD drives along. "The Redeemer will come to Zion, to those in Jacob who repent of their sins," declares the LORD. "As for me, this is my covenant with them," says the LORD. "My Spirit, who is on you, will not depart from you, and my words that I have put in your mouth will always be on your lips, on the lips of your children and on the lips of their descendants—from this time on and forever," says the LORD.

Isaiah 61:1–3: The Spirit of the Sovereign LORD is on me, because the LORD has anointed me to proclaim good news to the poor. He has sent me to bind up the brokenhearted, to proclaim freedom for the captives and release from darkness for the prisoners, to proclaim the year of the LORD's favor and the day of vengeance of our God, to comfort all who mourn, and provide for those who grieve in Zion—to bestow on them a crown of beauty instead of ashes, the oil of joy instead of mourning, and a garment of praise instead of a spirit of despair. They will be called oaks of righteousness, a planting of the LORD for the display of his splendor.

Isaiah 63:10: Yet they rebelled and grieved the Holy Spirit.

Ezekiel 1:12: Each one went straight ahead. Wherever the spirit would go, they would go, without turning as they went.

Ezekiel 1:20: Wherever the spirit would go, they would go, and the wheels would rise along with them, because the spirit of the living creatures was in the wheels.

Ezekiel 2:1–5: He said to me, "Son of man, stand up on your feet and I will speak to you." As he spoke, the Spirit came into me and raised me to my feet, and I heard him speaking to me. He said: "Son of man, I am sending you to the Israelites, to a rebellious nation that has rebelled against me; they and their ancestors have been in revolt against me to this very day. The people to whom I am sending you are obstinate and stubborn. Say to them, 'This is what the Sovereign LORD says.' And whether they listen or fail to listen— for they are a rebellious people—they will know that a prophet has been among them."

Ezekiel 3:12–13: Then the Spirit lifted me up, and I heard behind me a loud rumbling sound as the glory of the LORD rose from the place where it was standing. It was the sound of the wings of the living creatures brushing against each other and the sound of the wheels beside them, a loud rumbling sound.

Ezekiel 3:14: The Spirit then lifted me up and took me away, and I went in bitterness and in the anger of my spirit, with the strong hand of the Lord on me.

Ezekiel 11:1: Then the Spirit lifted me up and brought me to the gate of the house of the Lord that faces east.

Ezekiel 11:5: Then the Spirit of the Lord came on me, and he told me to say: "This is what the Lord says ..."

Ezekiel 11:22–25: Then the cherubim, with the wheels beside them, spread their wings, and the glory of the God of Israel was above them. The glory of the LORD went up from within the city and stopped above the mountain east of it. The Spirit lifted me up and brought me to the exiles in Babylonia in the vision given by the Spirit of God. Then the vision I had seen went up from me, and I told the exiles everything the LORD had shown me.

Ezekiel 36:22–32: Therefore, say to the Israelites, "This is what the Sovereign LORD says: It is not for your sake, people of Israel, that I am going to do these things, but for the sake of my holy name, which you have profaned among the nations where you have gone. I will show the holiness of my great name, which has been profaned among the nations, the name you have profaned among them. Then the nations will know that I am the LORD, declares the Sovereign LORD, when I am proved holy through you before their eyes. For I will take you out of the nations; I will gather you from all the countries and bring you back into your own land. I will sprinkle clean water on you, and you will be clean; I will cleanse you from all your impurities and from all your idols. I will give you a new heart and put a new spirit in you; I will remove from you your heart of stone and give you a heart of flesh. And I will put my Spirit in you and move you to follow my decrees and be careful to keep my laws. Then you will live in the land I gave your ancestors; you will be my people, and I will be your God. I will save you from all your uncleanness. I will call for the grain and make it plentiful and will not bring famine upon you. I will increase the fruit of the trees and the crops of the field, so that you will no longer suffer disgrace among the nations because of famine. Then you will remember your evil ways and wicked deeds, and you will loathe yourselves for your sins and detestable practices. I want you to know that I am not doing this for your sake, declares the Sovereign LORD. Be ashamed and disgraced for your conduct, people of Israel!'

Ezekiel 37:1–3: The hand of the Lord was on me, and he brought me out by the Spirit of the Lord and set me in the middle of a valley; it was full of bones. He led me back and forth among them, and I saw a great many bones on the floor of the valley, bones that were very dry. He asked me, "Son of man, can these bones live?" I said, "Sovereign Lord, you alone know."

Ezekiel 37:12–14: Therefore, prophesy and say to them: "This is what the Sovereign LORD says: My people, I am going to open your graves and bring you up from them; I will bring you back to the land of Israel. Then you, my people, will know that I am the LORD, when I open your graves and bring you up from them. I will put my Spirit in you and you will live, and I will settle you in your own land. Then you will know that I the LORD have spoken, and I have done it, declares the LORD."

Ezekiel 39:25–29: Therefore, this is what the Sovereign LORD says: I will now restore the fortunes of Jacob and will have compassion on all the people of Israel, and I will be zealous for my holy name. They will forget their shame and all the unfaithfulness they showed toward me when they lived in safety in their land with no one to make them afraid. When I have brought them back from the nations and have gathered them from the countries of their enemies, I will be proved holy through them in the sight of many nations. Then they will know that I am the LORD their God, for though I sent them into exile among the nations, I will gather them to their own land, not leaving any behind. I will no longer hide my face from them, for I will pour out my Spirit on the people of Israel, declares the Sovereign LORD.

Joel 2:28–32: And afterward, I will pour out my Spirit on all people. Your sons and daughters will prophesy, your old men will dream dreams, your young men will see visions. Even on my servants, both men and women, I will pour out my Spirit in those days. I will show wonders in the heavens and on the earth, blood and fire and billows of smoke. The sun will be turned to darkness and the moon to blood before the coming of the great and dreadful day of the LORD. And everyone who calls on the name of the LORD will be saved; for on Mount Zion and in Jerusalem there will be deliverance, as the LORD has said, even among the survivors whom the LORD calls.

Haggai 2:5: This is what I covenanted with you when you came out of Egypt. And my Spirit remains among you. Do not fear.

Zechariah 4:6: So he said to me, "This is the word of the LORD to Zerubbabel: 'Not by might nor by power, but by my Spirit,' says the LORD Almighty."

Zechariah 7:8–12: And the word of the LORD came again to Zechariah: "This is what the LORD Almighty said: 'Administer true justice; show mercy and compassion to one another. Do not oppress the widow or the fatherless, the foreigner or the poor. Do not plot evil against each other.' But they refused to pay attention; stubbornly they turned their backs and covered their ears. They made their hearts as hard as flint and would not listen to the law or to the words that the LORD Almighty had sent by his Spirit through the earlier prophets. So the LORD Almighty was very angry."

New Testament Scriptures Regarding the Holy Spirit

Matthew 1:18: This is how the birth of Jesus the Messiah came about: His mother Mary was pledged to be married to Joseph, but before they came together, she was found to be pregnant through the Holy Spirit.

Matthew 1:19–23: Because Joseph her husband was faithful to the law, and yet did not want to expose her to public disgrace, he had in mind to divorce her quietly. But after he had considered this, an angel of the Lord appeared to him in a dream and said, "Joseph son of David, do not be afraid to take Mary home as your wife, because what is conceived in her is from the Holy Spirit. She will give birth to a son, and you are to give him the name Jesus, because he will save his people from their sins." All this took place to fulfill what the Lord had said through the prophet: "The virgin will conceive and give birth to a son, and they will call him Immanuel [which means "God with us"]."

Matthew 3:7–12: But when he (John the Baptist) saw many of the Pharisees and Sadducees coming to where he was baptizing, he said to them: "You brood of vipers! Who warned you to flee from the coming wrath? Produce fruit in keeping with repentance. And do not think you can say to yourselves, 'We have Abraham as our father.' I tell you that out of these stones God can raise up children for Abraham. The ax is already at the root of the trees, and every tree that does not produce good fruit will be cut down and thrown into the fire. I baptize you with water for repentance. But after me comes one who is more powerful than I, whose sandals I am not worthy to carry. He will baptize you with the Holy Spirit and fire. His winnowing fork is in his hand, and he will clear his threshing floor, gathering his wheat into the barn and burning up the chaff with unquenchable fire."

Matthew 3:13–17: Then Jesus came from Galilee to the Jordan to be baptized by John. But John tried to deter him, saying, "I need to be baptized by you, and do you come to me?" Jesus replied, "Let it be so now; it is proper for us to do this to fulfill all righteousness." Then John consented. As soon as Jesus was baptized, he went up out of the water. At that moment heaven was opened, and he saw the Spirit of God descending like a dove and alighting on him. And a voice from heaven said, "This is my Son, whom I love; with him I am well pleased."

Matthew 4:1: Then Jesus was led by the Spirit into the wilderness to be tempted by the devil.

Matthew 10:19–20: But when they arrest you, do not worry about what to say or how to say it. At that time you will be given what to say, for it will not be you speaking, but the Spirit of your Father speaking through you.

Matthew 12:15–21: Aware of this, Jesus withdrew from that place. A large crowd followed him, and he healed all who were ill. He warned them not to tell others about him. This was to fulfill what was spoken through the prophet Isaiah: "Here is my servant whom I have chosen, the one I love, in whom I delight; I will put my Spirit on him, and he will proclaim justice to the nations. He will not quarrel or cry out; no one will hear his voice in the streets. A bruised reed he will not break, and a smoldering wick he will not snuff out, till he has brought justice through to victory. In his name the nations will put their hope."

Matthew 12:24–28: But when the Pharisees heard this, they said, "It is only by Beelzebul, the prince of demons, that this fellow drives out demons." Jesus knew their thoughts and said to them, "Every kingdom divided against itself will be ruined, and every city or household divided against itself will not stand. If Satan drives out Satan, he is divided against himself. How then can his kingdom stand? And if I drive out demons by Beelzebul, by whom do your people drive them out? So then, they will be your judges. But if it is by the Spirit of God that I drive out demons, then the kingdom of God has come upon you."

Matthew 12:30–32: Whoever is not with me is against me, and whoever does not gather with me scatters. And so I tell you, every kind of sin and slander can be forgiven, but blasphemy against the Spirit will not be forgiven. Anyone who speaks a word against the Son of Man will be forgiven, but anyone who speaks against the Holy Spirit will not be forgiven, either in this age or in the age to come.

Matthew 28:16–19: Then the eleven disciples went to Galilee, to the mountain where Jesus had told them to go. When they saw him, they worshiped him; but some doubted. Then Jesus came to them and said, "All authority in heaven and on earth has been given to me. Therefore go and make disciples of all nations, baptizing them in the name of the Father and of the Son and of the Holy Spirit, and teaching them to obey everything I have commanded you. And surely I am with you always, to the very end of the age."

Mark 1:1–8: The beginning of the good news about Jesus the Messiah, the Son of God, as it is written in Isaiah the prophet: "I will send my messenger ahead of you, who will prepare your way— a voice of one calling in the wilderness, 'Prepare the way for the Lord, make straight paths for him.'" And so John the Baptist appeared in the wilderness, preaching a baptism of repentance for the forgiveness of sins. The whole Judean countryside and all the people of Jerusalem went out to him. Confessing their sins, they were baptized by him in the Jordan River. John wore clothing made of camel's hair, with a leather belt around his waist, and he ate locusts and wild honey. And this was his message: "After me comes the one more powerful than I, the straps of whose sandals I am not worthy to stoop down and untie. I baptize you with water, but he will baptize you with the Holy Spirit."

Mark 1:9–11: At that time Jesus came from Nazareth in Galilee and was baptized by John in the Jordan. Just as Jesus was coming up out of the water, he saw heaven being torn open and the Spirit descending on him like a dove. And a voice came from heaven: "You are my Son, whom I love; with you I am well pleased."

Mark 1:12–13: At once the Spirit sent him out into the wilderness, and he was in the wilderness forty days, being tempted by Satan. He was with the wild animals, and angels attended him.

Mark 12:35–37: While Jesus was teaching in the temple courts, he asked, "Why do the teachers of the law say that the Messiah is the son of David? David himself, speaking by the Holy Spirit, declared: 'The Lord said to my Lord: "Sit at my right hand until I put your enemies under your feet."' David himself calls him 'Lord.' How then can he be his son?" The large crowd listened to him with delight.

Luke 1:11–17: Then an angel of the Lord appeared to him, standing at the right side of the altar of incense. When Zechariah saw him, he was startled and was gripped with fear. But the angel said to him: "Do not be afraid, Zechariah; your prayer has been heard. Your wife Elizabeth will bear you a son, and you are to call him John. He will be a joy and delight to you, and many will rejoice because of his birth, for he will be great in the sight of the Lord. He is never to take wine or other fermented drink, and he will be filled with the Holy Spirit even before he is born. He will bring back many of the people of Israel to the Lord their God. And he will go on before the Lord, in the spirit and power of Elijah, to turn the hearts of the parents to their children and the disobedient to the wisdom of the righteous—to make ready a people prepared for the Lord."

Luke 1:28–38: The angel went to her and said, "Greetings, you who are highly favored! The Lord is with you." Mary was greatly troubled at his words and wondered what kind of greeting this might be. But the angel said to her, "Do not be afraid, Mary; you have found favor with God. You will conceive and give birth to a son, and you are to call him Jesus. He will be great and will be called the Son of the Most High. The Lord God will give him the throne of his father David, and he will reign over Jacob's descendants forever; his kingdom will never end." "How will this be," Mary asked the angel, "since I am a virgin?" The angel answered, "The Holy Spirit will come on you, and the power of the Most High will overshadow you. So the holy one to be born will be called the Son of God. Even Elizabeth your relative is going to have a child in her old age, and she who was said to be unable to conceive is in her sixth month. For no word from God will ever fail." "I am the Lord's servant," Mary answered. "May it be to me as you have said." Then the angel left her.

Luke 1:39–45: At that time Mary got ready and hurried to a town in the hill country of Judea, where she entered Zechariah's home and greeted Elizabeth. When Elizabeth heard Mary's greeting, the baby leaped in her womb, and Elizabeth was filled with the Holy Spirit. In a loud voice she exclaimed: "Blessed are you among women, and blessed is the child you will bear! But why am I so favored, that the mother of my Lord should come to me? As soon as the sound of your greeting reached my ears, the baby in my womb leaped for joy. Blessed is she who has believed that the Lord would fulfill his promises to her!"

Luke 1:57–67: When it was time for Elizabeth to have her baby, she gave birth to a son. Her neighbors and relatives heard that the Lord had shown her great mercy, and they shared her joy. On the eighth day they came to circumcise the child, and they were going to name him after his father Zechariah, but his mother spoke up and said, "No! He is to be called John." They said to her, "There is no one among your relatives who has that name. " Then they made signs to his father, to find out what he would like to name the child.

He asked for a writing tablet, and to everyone's astonishment he wrote, "His name is John." Immediately his mouth was opened and his tongue set free, and he began to speak, praising God. All the neighbors were filled with awe, and throughout the hill country of Judea people were talking about all these things. Everyone who heard this wondered about it, asking, "What then is this child going to be?" For the Lord's hand was with him. His father Zechariah was filled with the Holy Spirit and prophesied. [See verses 68–80.]

Luke 2:21–32: On the eighth day, when it was time to circumcise the child, he was named Jesus, the name the angel had given him before he was conceived. When the time came for the purification rites required by the Law of Moses, Joseph and Mary took him to Jerusalem to present him to the Lord (as it is written in the Law of the Lord, "Every firstborn male is to be consecrated to the Lord"), and to offer a sacrifice in keeping with what is said in the Law of the Lord: "a pair of doves or two young pigeons." Now there was a man in Jerusalem called Simeon, who was righteous and devout. He was waiting for the consolation of Israel, and the Holy Spirit was on him. It had been revealed to him by the Holy Spirit that he would not die before he had seen the Lord's Messiah. Moved by the Spirit, he went into the temple courts. When the parents brought in the child Jesus to do for him what the custom of the Law required, Simeon took him in his arms and praised God, saying: "Sovereign Lord, as you have promised, you may now dismiss your servant in peace. For my eyes have seen your salvation, which you have prepared in the sight of all nations: a light for revelation to the Gentiles, and the glory of your people Israel."

Luke 3:15–18: The people were waiting expectantly and were all wondering in their hearts if John might possibly be the Messiah. John answered them all, "I baptize you with water. But one who is more powerful than I will come, the straps of whose sandals I am not worthy to untie. He will baptize you with the Holy Spirit and fire. His winnowing fork is in his hand to clear his threshing floor and to gather the wheat into his barn, but he will burn up the chaff with unquenchable fire." And with many other words John exhorted the people and proclaimed the good news to them.

Luke 3:21–23: When all the people were being baptized, Jesus was baptized too. And as he was praying, heaven was opened and the Holy Spirit descended on him in bodily form like a dove. And a voice came from heaven: "You are my Son, whom I love; with you I am well pleased." Now Jesus himself was about thirty years old when he began his ministry.

Luke 4:1–2: Jesus, full of the Holy Spirit, left the Jordan and was led by the Spirit into the wilderness, where for forty days he was tempted by the devil. He ate nothing during those days, and at the end of them he was hungry.

Luke 4:14–15: Jesus returned to Galilee in the power of the Spirit, and news about him spread through the whole countryside. He was teaching in their synagogues, and everyone praised him.

Luke 4: 16–19: He went to Nazareth, where he had been brought up, and on the Sabbath day he went into the synagogue, as was his custom. He stood up to read, and the scroll of the prophet Isaiah was handed to him. Unrolling it, he found the place where it is written: "The Spirit of the Lord is on me, because he has anointed me to proclaim good news to the poor. He has sent me to proclaim freedom for the prisoners and recovery of sight for the blind, to set the oppressed free, to proclaim the year of the Lord's favor."

Luke 10:17–24: The seventy-two returned with joy and said, "Lord, even the demons submit to us in your name." He replied, "I saw Satan fall like lightning from heaven. I have given you authority to trample on snakes and scorpions and to overcome all the power of the enemy; nothing will harm you. However, do not rejoice that the spirits submit to you, but rejoice that your names are written in heaven." At that time Jesus, full of joy through the Holy Spirit, said, "I praise you, Father, Lord of heaven and earth, because you have hidden these things from the wise and learned, and revealed them to little children. Yes, Father, for this is what you were pleased to do. All things have been committed to me by my Father. No one knows who the Son is except the Father, and no one knows who the Father is except the Son and those to whom the Son chooses to reveal him." Then he turned to his disciples and said privately, "Blessed are the eyes that see what you see. For I tell you that many prophets and kings wanted to see what you see but did not see it, and to hear what you hear but did not hear it."

Luke 11:1–13: One day Jesus was praying in a certain place. When he finished, one of his disciples said to him, "Lord, teach us to pray, just as John taught his disciples." He said to them, "When you pray, say: "'Father, hallowed be your name, your kingdom come. Give us each day our daily bread. Forgive us our sins, for we also forgive everyone who sins against us. And lead us not into temptation.'" Then Jesus said to them, "Suppose you have a friend, and you go to him at midnight and say, 'Friend, lend me three loaves of bread; a friend of mine on a journey has come to me, and I have no food to offer him.' And suppose the one inside answers, 'Don't bother me. The door is already locked, and my children and I are in bed. I can't get up and give you anything.' I tell you, even though he will not get up and give you the bread because of friendship, yet because of your shameless audacity he will surely get up and give you as much as you need. So I say to you: Ask and it will be given to you; seek and you will find; knock and the door will be opened to you. For everyone who asks receives; the one who seeks finds; and to the one who knocks, the door will be opened. Which of you fathers, if your son asks for a fish, will give him a snake instead? Or if he asks for an egg, will give him a scorpion? If you then, though you are evil, know how to give good gifts to your children, how much more will your Father in heaven give the Holy Spirit to those who ask him!"

Luke 12:1–12: Meanwhile, when a crowd of many thousands had gathered, so that they were trampling on one another, Jesus began to speak first to his disciples, saying: "Be on your guard against the yeast of the Pharisees, which is hypocrisy. There is nothing concealed that will not be disclosed, or hidden that will not be made known. What you have said in the dark will be heard in the daylight, and what you have whispered in the ear in the inner rooms will be proclaimed from the roofs. I tell you, my friends, do not be afraid of those who kill the body and after that can do no more. But I will show you whom you should fear: Fear him who, after your body has been killed, has authority to throw you into hell. Yes, I tell you, fear him. Are not five sparrows sold for two pennies? Yet not one of them is forgotten by God. Indeed, the very hairs of your head are all numbered. Don't be afraid; you are worth more than many sparrows.

"I tell you, whoever publicly acknowledges me before others, the Son of Man will also acknowledge before the angels of God. But whoever disowns me before others will be disowned before the angels of God. And everyone who speaks a word against the Son of Man will be forgiven, but anyone who blasphemes against the Holy Spirit will not be forgiven. "When you are brought before synagogues, rulers and authorities, do not worry about how you will defend yourselves or what you will say, for the Holy Spirit will teach you at that time what you should say."

Luke 21:14–15: But make up your mind not to worry beforehand how you will defend yourselves. For I will give you words and wisdom that none of your adversaries will be able to resist or contradict. [Note: Jesus here ensures the presence of the Holy Spirit, confirming his promise given to the disciples in John 14:15–17, iterating with "I will give you words and wisdom."]

Luke 24:44–49: He said to them, "This is what I told you while I was still with you: Everything must be fulfilled that is written about me in the Law of Moses, the Prophets and the Psalms. "Then he opened their minds so they could understand the Scriptures. He told them, "This is what is written: The Messiah will suffer and rise from the dead on the third day, and repentance for the forgiveness of sins will be preached in his name to all nations, beginning at Jerusalem. You are witnesses of these things. I am going to send you what my Father has promised; but stay in the city until you have been clothed with power from on high." [Note: Verse 49 states, "I am going to send you what my Father has promised; but stay in the city until you have been clothed with power from on high." (See confirmation of Jesus's promise in John 14:15–17 and Acts 1: 1–8.)]

John 1:29–34: The next day John saw Jesus coming toward him and said, "Look, the Lamb of God, who takes away the sin of the world! This is the one I meant when I said, 'A man who comes after me has surpassed me because he was before me.' I myself did not know him, but the reason I came baptizing with water was that he might be revealed to Israel." Then John gave this testimony: "I saw the Spirit come down from heaven as a dove and remain on him. And I myself did not know him, but the one who sent me to baptize with water told me, 'The man on whom you see the Spirit come down and remain is the one who will baptize with the Holy Spirit.' I have seen and I testify that this is God's Chosen One."

John 3:27–36: To this John replied, "A person can receive only what is given them from heaven. You yourselves can testify that I said, 'I am not the Messiah but am sent ahead of him.' The bride belongs to the bridegroom. The friend who attends the bridegroom waits and listens for him, and is full of joy when he hears the bridegroom's voice. That joy is mine, and it is now complete. He must become greater; I must become less." The one who comes from above is above all; the one who is from the earth belongs to the earth, and speaks as one from the earth. The one who comes from heaven is above all. He testifies to what he has seen and heard, but no one accepts his testimony. Whoever has accepted it has certified that God is truthful. For the one whom God has sent speaks the words of God, for God gives the Spirit without limit. The Father loves the Son and has placed everything in his hands. Whoever believes in the Son has eternal life, but whoever rejects the Son will not see life, for God's wrath remains on them.

John 4:13–14: Jesus answered, "Everyone who drinks this water will be thirsty again, but whoever drinks the water I give them will never thirst. Indeed, the water I give them will become in them a spring of water welling up to eternal life." [Note: Jesus is here referring to the indwelling Holy Spirit he promised in John 14:15–17, Acts 1:1–8, and John 7:37–39.]

John 4:21–24: "Woman," Jesus replied, "believe me, a time is coming when you will worship the Father neither on this mountain nor in Jerusalem. You Samaritans worship what you do not know; we worship what we do know, for salvation is from the Jews. Yet a time is coming and has now come when the true worshipers will worship the Father in the Spirit and in truth, for they are the kind of worshipers the Father seeks. God is spirit, and his worshipers must worship in the Spirit and in truth."

John 5:24–27: Very truly I tell you, whoever hears my word and believes him who sent me has eternal life and will not be judged but has crossed over from death to life. Very truly I tell you, a time is coming and has now come when the dead will hear the voice of the Son of God and those who hear will live. For as the Father has life in himself, so he has granted the Son also to have life in himself. And he has given him authority to judge because he is the Son of Man. [Note: This also confirms the Holy Spirit in the redeemed of Christ Jesus.]

John 6: 35–40: Then Jesus declared, "I am the bread of life. Whoever comes to me will never go hungry, and whoever believes in me will never be thirsty. But as I told you, you have seen me and still you do not believe. All those the Father gives me will come to me, and whoever comes to me I will never drive away. For I have come down from heaven not to do my will but to do the will of him who sent me. And this is the will of him who sent me, that I shall lose none of all those he has given me, but raise them up at the last day. For my Father's will is that everyone who looks to the Son and believes in him shall have eternal life, and I will raise them up at the last day." [Note: "The bread of life" is the Spirit of Jesus indwelling his redeemed.]

John 6:44–51: No one can come to me unless the Father who sent me draws them, and I will raise them up at the last day. It is written in the Prophets: "They will all be taught by God." Everyone who has heard the Father and learned from him comes to me. No one has seen the Father except the one who is from God; only he has seen the Father. Very truly I tell you, the one who believes has eternal life. I am the bread of life. Your ancestors ate the manna in the wilderness, yet they died. But here is the bread that comes down from heaven, which anyone may eat and not die. I am the living bread that came down from heaven. Whoever eats this bread will live forever. This bread is my flesh, which I will give for the life of the world.

John 6:63: The Spirit gives life; the flesh counts for nothing. The words I have spoken to you—they are full of the Spirit and life.

John 7:33–39: Jesus said, "I am with you for only a short time, and then I am going to the one who sent me. You will look for me, but you will not find me; and where I am, you cannot come." The Jews said to one another, "Where does this man intend to go that we cannot find him? Will he go where our people live scattered among the Greeks, and teach the Greeks? What did he mean when he said, 'You will look for me, but you will not find me,' and 'Where I am, you cannot come'?" On the last and greatest day of the festival, Jesus stood and said in a loud voice, "Let anyone who is thirsty come to me and drink. Whoever believes in me, as Scripture has said, rivers of living water will flow from within them." By this he meant the Spirit, whom those who believed in him were later to receive. Up to that time the Spirit had not been given, since Jesus had not yet been glorified.

John 8:12: When Jesus spoke again to the people, he said, "I am the light of the world. Whoever follows me will never walk in darkness, but will have the light of life." [Note: Here Jesus also confirms the Holy Spirit as "Light". Jesus's being the "light of the world" iterates the Holy Spirit's illumination through himself and his redeemed.]

John 10:14–18: I am the good shepherd; I know my sheep and my sheep know me— just as the Father knows me and I know the Father—and I lay down my life for the sheep. I have other sheep that are not of this sheep pen. I must bring them also. They too will listen to my voice, and there shall be one flock and one shepherd. The reason my Father loves me is that I lay down my life—only to take it up again. No one takes it from me, but I lay it down of my own accord. I have authority to lay it down and authority to take it up again. This command I received from my Father. [Note: Jesus not only indicates he is the "shepherd" to those listening but also iterates his being "shepherd" to all the redeemed through the Holy Spirit. He also iterates his authority to raise up his body by the power of the Spirit.]

John 11:23–27: Jesus said to her, "Your brother will rise again." Martha answered, "I know he will rise again in the resurrection at the last day." Jesus said to her, "I am the resurrection and the life. The one who believes in me will live, even though they die; and whoever lives by believing in me will never die. Do you believe this?" "Yes, Lord," she replied, "I believe that you are the Messiah, the Son of God, who is to come into the world." [Note: Jesus confirms the Holy Spirit of power, as he proclaims himself to be "the resurrection and the life."]

John 14:15–19: If you love me, keep my commands. And I will ask the Father, and he will give you another advocate to help you and be with you forever—the Spirit of truth. The world cannot accept him, because it neither sees him nor knows him. But you know him, for he lives with you and will be in you. I will not leave you as orphans; I will come to you. Before long, the world will not see me anymore, but you will see me. Because I live, you also will live.

John 14:20: On that day you will realize that I am in my Father, and you are in me, and I am in you. [Note: The Father and the Son living in the redeemed also includes and confirms the Holy Spirit living in the same.]

John 14:23: Jesus replied, "Anyone who loves me will obey my teaching. My Father will love them, and we will come to them and make our home with them." [See note on John 14:20.]

John 14:25–27: All this I have spoken while still with you. But the Advocate, the Holy Spirit, whom the Father will send in my name, will teach you all things and will remind you of everything I have said to you. Peace I leave with you; my peace I give you. I do not give to you as the world gives. Do not let your hearts be troubled and do not be afraid.

John 15:16–17: You did not choose me, but I chose you and appointed you so that you might go and bear fruit—fruit that will last—and so that whatever you ask in my name the Father will give you. This is my command: Love each other. [Note: Refer to Galatians 5:22–23 as to the "fruit" to which Jesus points.]

John 15:26–27: When the Advocate comes, whom I will send to you from the Father—the Spirit of truth who goes out from the Father—he will testify about me. And you also must testify, for you have been with me from the beginning. [Note: The Advocate is the Holy Spirit.]

John 16:7–11: But very truly I tell you, it is for your good that I am going away. Unless I go away, the Advocate will not come to you; but if I go, I will send him to you. When he comes, he will prove the world to be in the wrong about sin and righteousness and judgment: about sin, because people do not believe in me; about righteousness, because I am going to the Father, where you can see me no longer; and about judgment, because the prince of this world now stands condemned. [See note on John 15:26–27.]

John 16:13–15: But when he, the Spirit of truth, comes, he will guide you into all the truth. He will not speak on his own; he will speak only what he hears, and he will tell you what is yet to come. He will glorify me because it is from me that he will receive what he will make known to you. All that belongs to the Father is mine. That is why I said the Spirit will receive from me what he will make known to you.

John 20: 19–23: On the evening of that first day of the week, when the disciples were together, with the doors locked for fear of the Jewish leaders, Jesus came and stood among them and said, "Peace be with you!" After he said this, he showed them his hands and side. The disciples were overjoyed when they saw the Lord. Again Jesus said, "Peace be with you! As the Father has sent me, I am sending you." And with that he breathed on them and said, "Receive the Holy Spirit. If you forgive anyone's sins, their sins are forgiven; if you do not forgive them, they are not forgiven." [Note: Jesus breathed on the disciples and said "Receive the Holy Spirit." This was initial to them. Just prior to and on the Day of Pentecost, per Jesus's instructions (found in Acts 1:4, 8), the disciples and subsequently the "whosoever" were indwelled with the Holy Spirit. This began the universal indwelling of the redeemed in Jesus, by the Holy Spirit, that God has in place in this age of grace.]

Acts 1:2–5: Until the day he was taken up to heaven, after giving instructions through the Holy Spirit to the apostles he had chosen. After his suffering, he presented himself to them and gave many convincing proofs that he was alive. He appeared to them over a period of forty days and spoke about the kingdom of God. On one occasion, while he was eating with them, he gave them this command: "Do not leave Jerusalem, but wait for the gift my Father promised, which you have heard me speak about. For John baptized with water, but in a few days you will be baptized with the Holy Spirit."

Acts 1:8: But you will receive power when the Holy Spirit comes on you; and you will be my witnesses in Jerusalem, and in all Judea and Samaria, and to the ends of the earth." [Note: "But you will receive power when the Holy Spirit comes on you" confirms Jesus's command of the full indwelling power of the Holy Spirit in whom he will reside. This was carried out as the initial universal indwelling of the redeemed of Christ, thus empowering the recipients to be universal fruit-bearing representatives of Christ, as all of Christ's redeemed are today. The beginning of the universal indwelling began precisely on the Day of Pentecost, as was promised and carries on with each and every one of Jesus's redeemed.]

Acts 1:15–17: In those days Peter stood up among the believers (a group numbering about a hundred and twenty) and said, "Brothers and sisters, the Scripture had to be fulfilled in which the Holy Spirit spoke long ago through David concerning Judas, who served as guide for those who arrested Jesus. He was one of our number and shared in our ministry." [See verses 18–26.]

Acts 2:1–3: When the day of Pentecost came, they were all together in one place. Suddenly a sound like the blowing of a violent wind came from heaven and filled the whole house where they were sitting. They saw what seemed to be tongues of fire that separated and came to rest on each of them.

Acts 2:4: All of them were filled with the Holy Spirit and began to speak in other tongues as the Spirit enabled them. [Note: A great deal of controversy has arisen from this one verse. With a completely clear understanding—through the scriptures—and examined for complete content, it is seen that the Holy Spirit indwelled the group gathered in the room and has also continued this ministry of indwelling each and every redeemed believer as Jesus has faithfully promised. "To speak in other tongues as the Spirit enabled them" means just that. The group was enabled by the Holy Spirit on that particular occasion to bring about awareness of his presence. And with this being done, those in the outside crowd who would listen in belief were brought to an understanding, as explained by Peter and confirmed by the Holy Spirit, that in order to be saved, "repentance" was required, thus bringing about the immediate forgiveness of their sins through the shed blood of Jesus, and this bringing instantaneous and permanent indwelling of the Holy Spirit within the cleansed soul of each and every believer. (See Acts 2:5–41 for the paramount reason of the indwelling Holy Spirit.)

Please further note that should you have a question about the gift of tongues as is referred to in God's Word, it would greatly benefit you to seek the Holy Spirit's guidance. He, through the Word of God, will guide you into all truth. 1 Corinthians 12–14 is one of the areas of the Bible where much emphasis has been focused regarding spiritual gifts. There is no doubt the Holy Spirit does have the power to bestow upon any Christian, "as He enables," the gift of tongues, just as he does any other spiritual gift. It is completely the Holy Spirit who determines this gift. It is not up to a fellow Christian to persuade you to acquire a special blessing or to get the Spirit. The Holy Spirit, upon your redemption in Jesus Christ, took up permanent residence within your saved soul immediately upon your redemption. From this point forward, the Holy Spirit will truly act through you and use you to witness to the world your blessed Savior Jesus Christ, while you give thanks and glory to the Father. The absolute truth of the plan of God is found in the Word of God—the Bible. No other source is absolutely viable, regardless the dedication of God's redeemed. (See plainly the clear picture in Acts 2: 37–41.)].

Acts 2:37–41: When the people heard this, they were cut to the heart and said to Peter and the other apostles, "Brothers, what shall we do?" Peter replied, "Repent and be baptized, every one of you, in the name of Jesus Christ for the forgiveness of your sins. And you will receive the gift of the Holy Spirit. The promise is for you and your children and for all who are far off—for all whom the Lord our God will call." With many other words he warned them; and he pleaded with them, "Save yourselves from this corrupt generation." Those who accepted his message were baptized, and about three thousand were added to their number that day.

Acts 4:1–13: The priests and the captain of the temple guard and the Sadducees came up to Peter and John while they were speaking to the people. They were greatly disturbed because the apostles were teaching the people, proclaiming in Jesus the resurrection of the dead. They seized Peter and John and, because it was evening, they put them in jail until the next day. But many who heard the message believed; so the number of men who believed grew to about five thousand.

The next day the rulers, the elders and the teachers of the law met in Jerusalem. Annas the high priest was there, and so were Caiaphas, John, Alexander and others of the high priest's family. They had Peter and John brought before them and began to question them: "By what power or what name did you do this?" Then Peter, filled with the Holy Spirit, said to them: "Rulers and elders of the people! If we are being called to account today for an act of kindness shown to a man who was lame and are being asked how he was healed, then know this, you and all the people of Israel: It is by the name of Jesus Christ of Nazareth, whom you crucified but whom God raised from the dead, that this man stands before you healed. Jesus is 'the stone you builders rejected, which has become the cornerstone.' Salvation is found in no one else, for there is no other name under heaven given to mankind by which we must be saved." When they saw the courage of Peter and John and realized that they were unschooled, ordinary men, they were astonished and they took note that these men had been with Jesus. [Note: It is here where the Christian must realize that the Holy Spirit, on the promised Day of Pentecost, took up permanent residence in Peter and all the rest who believed that day and beyond. The word "filled" leads to the truth that the Holy Spirit fills the Christian as he determines. The Holy Spirit does not come and go in the Christian. He empowers as he Jesus promised he would do. Refer back to Luke 21:15 to confirm. It is very important to understand the truth of God's promise and how it intertwines throughout his Word and in all Christian lives. Also look at Ephesians 5:15–21].

Acts 4:23–31: On their release, Peter and John went back to their own people and reported all that the chief priests and the elders had said to them. When they heard this, they raised their voices together in prayer to God. "Sovereign Lord," they said, "you made the heavens and the earth and the sea, and everything in them. You spoke by the Holy Spirit through the mouth of your servant, our father David: 'Why do the nations rage and the peoples plot in vain? The kings of the earth rise up and the rulers band together against the Lord and against his anointed one.' Indeed Herod and Pontius Pilate met together with the Gentiles and the people of Israel in this city to conspire against your holy servant Jesus, whom you anointed. They did what your power and will had decided beforehand should happen. Now, Lord, consider their threats and enable your servants to speak your word with great boldness. Stretch out your hand to heal and perform signs and wonders through the name of your holy servant Jesus." After they prayed, the place where they were meeting was shaken. And they were all filled with the Holy Spirit and spoke the word of God boldly. [Concerning "filled," see note on Acts 4:1–13.]

Acts 5:1–11: Now a man named Ananias, together with his wife Sapphira, also sold a piece of property. With his wife's full knowledge he kept back part of the money for himself, but brought the rest and put it at the apostles' feet. Then Peter said, "Ananias, how is it that Satan has so filled your heart that you have lied to the Holy Spirit and have kept for yourself some of the money you received for the land? Didn't it belong to you before it was sold? And after it was sold, wasn't the money at your disposal? What made you think of doing such a thing? You have not lied just to human beings but to God." When Ananias heard this, he fell down and died. And great fear seized all who heard what had happened. Then some young men came forward, wrapped up his body, and carried him out and buried him. About three hours later his wife came in, not knowing what had happened. Peter asked her, "Tell me, is this the price you and Ananias got for the land?" "Yes," she said, "that is the price." Peter said to her, "How could you conspire to test the Spirit of the

Lord? Listen! The feet of the men who buried your husband are at the door, and they will carry you out also." At that moment she fell down at his feet and died. Then the young men came in and, finding her dead, carried her out and buried her beside her husband. Great fear seized the whole church and all who heard about these events.

Acts 5:25–32: Then someone came and said, "Look! The men you put in jail are standing in the temple courts teaching the people." At that, the captain went with his officers and brought the apostles. They did not use force, because they feared that the people would stone them. The apostles were brought in and made to appear before the Sanhedrin to be questioned by the high priest. "We gave you strict orders not to teach in this name," he said. "Yet you have filled Jerusalem with your teaching and are determined to make us guilty of this man's blood." Peter and the other apostles replied: "We must obey God rather than human beings! The God of our ancestors raised Jesus from the dead—whom you killed by hanging him on a cross. God exalted him to his own right hand as Prince and Savior that he might bring Israel to repentance and forgive their sins. We are witnesses of these things, and so is the Holy Spirit, whom God has given to those who obey him."

Acts 6:1–7: In those days when the number of disciples was increasing, the Hellenistic Jews among them complained against the Hebraic Jews because their widows were being overlooked in the daily distribution of food. So the Twelve gathered all the disciples together and said, "It would not be right for us to neglect the ministry of the word of God in order to wait on tables. Brothers and sisters, choose seven men from among you who are known to be full of the Spirit and wisdom. We will turn this responsibility over to them and will give our attention to prayer and the ministry of the word." This proposal pleased the whole group. They chose Stephen, a man full of faith and of the Holy Spirit; also Philip, Procorus, Nicanor, Timon, Parmenas, and Nicolas from Antioch, a convert to Judaism. They presented these men to the apostles, who prayed and laid their hands on them. So the word of God spread. The number of disciples in Jerusalem increased rapidly, and a large number of priests became obedient to the faith.

Acts 6:8−10: Now Stephen, a man full of God's grace and power, performed great wonders and signs among the people. Opposition arose, however, from members of the Synagogue of the Freedmen (as it was called)—Jews of Cyrene and Alexandria as well as the provinces of Cilicia and Asia—who began to argue with Stephen. But they could not stand up against the wisdom the Spirit gave him as he spoke.

Acts 7:44−53: Our ancestors had the tabernacle of the covenant law with them in the wilderness. It had been made as God directed Moses, according to the pattern he had seen. After receiving the tabernacle, our ancestors under Joshua brought it with them when they took the land from the nations God drove out before them. It remained in the land until the time of David, who enjoyed God's favor and asked that he might provide a dwelling place for the God of Jacob. But it was Solomon who built a house for him. However, the Most High does not live in houses made by human hands. As the prophet says: "Heaven is my throne, and the earth is my footstool. What kind of house will you build for me? says the Lord. Or where will my resting place be? Has not my hand made all these things?" You stiff-necked people! Your hearts and ears are still uncircumcised. You are just like your ancestors: You always resist the Holy Spirit! Was there ever a prophet your ancestors did not persecute? They even killed those who predicted the coming of the Righteous One. And now you have betrayed and murdered him— you who have received the law that was given through angels but have not obeyed it.

Acts 8:14−17: When the apostles in Jerusalem heard that Samaria had accepted the word of God, they sent Peter and John to Samaria. When they arrived, they prayed for the new believers there that they might receive the Holy Spirit, because the Holy Spirit had not yet come on any of them; they had simply been baptized in the name of the Lord Jesus. Then Peter and John placed their hands on them, and they received the Holy Spirit.

Acts 8:26–31: Now an angel of the Lord said to Philip, "Go south to the road—the desert road—that goes down from Jerusalem to Gaza." So he started out, and on his way he met an Ethiopian eunuch, an important official in charge of all the treasury of the Kandake (which means "queen of the Ethiopians"). This man had gone to Jerusalem to worship, and on his way home was sitting in his chariot reading the Book of Isaiah the prophet. The Spirit told Philip, "Go to that chariot and stay near it." Then Philip ran up to the chariot and heard the man reading Isaiah the prophet. "Do you understand what you are reading?" Philip asked. "How can I," he said, "unless someone explains it to me?" So he invited Philip to come up and sit with him.

Acts 8:34–39: The eunuch asked Philip, "Tell me, please, who is the prophet talking about, himself or someone else?" Then Philip began with that very passage of Scripture and told him the good news about Jesus. As they traveled along the road, they came to some water and the eunuch said, "Look, here is water. What can stand in the way of my being baptized?" And he gave orders to stop the chariot. Then both Philip and the eunuch went down into the water and Philip baptized him. When they came up out of the water, the Spirit of the Lord suddenly took Philip away, and the eunuch did not see him again, but went on his way rejoicing.

Acts 9:10–12 and 15–18: In Damascus there was a disciple named Ananias. The Lord called to him in a vision, "Ananias!" "Yes, Lord," he answered. The Lord told him, "Go to the house of Judas on Straight Street and ask for a man from Tarsus named Saul, for he is praying. In a vision he has seen a man named Ananias come and place his hands on him to restore his sight." But the Lord said to Ananias, "Go! This man is my chosen instrument to proclaim my name to the Gentiles and their kings and to the people of Israel. I will show him how much he must suffer for my name." Then

Ananias went to the house and entered it. Placing his hands on Saul, he said, "Brother Saul, the Lord—Jesus, who appeared to you on the road as you were coming here—has sent me so that you may see again and be filled with the Holy Spirit." Immediately, something like scales fell from Saul's eyes, and he could see again. He got up and was baptized.

Acts 9:23–31: After many days had gone by, there was a conspiracy among the Jews to kill him, but Saul learned of their plan. Day and night they kept close watch on the city gates in order to kill him. But his followers took him by night and lowered him in a basket through an opening in the wall. When he came to Jerusalem, he tried to join the disciples, but they were all afraid of him, not believing that he really was a disciple. But Barnabas took him and brought him to the apostles. He told them how Saul on his journey had seen the Lord and that the Lord had spoken to him, and how in Damascus he had preached fearlessly in the name of Jesus. So Saul stayed with them and moved about freely in Jerusalem, speaking boldly in the name of the Lord. He talked and debated with the Hellenistic Jews, but they tried to kill him. When the believers learned of this, they took him down to Caesarea and sent him off to Tarsus. Then the church throughout Judea, Galilee and Samaria enjoyed a time of peace and was strengthened. Living in the fear of the Lord and encouraged by the Holy Spirit, it increased in numbers.

Acts 10:19–23: While Peter was still thinking about the vision, the Spirit said to him, "Simon, three men are looking for you. So get up and go downstairs. Do not hesitate to go with them, for I have sent them." Peter went down and said to the men, "I'm the one you're looking for. Why have you come?" The men replied, "We have come from Cornelius the centurion. He is a righteous and God-fearing man, who is respected by all the Jewish people. A holy angel told him to ask you to come to his house so that he could hear what you have to say." Then Peter invited the men into the house to be his guests.

Acts 10:24–38: The following day he arrived in Caesarea. Cornelius was expecting them and had called together his relatives and close friends. As Peter entered the house, Cornelius met him and fell at his feet in reverence. But Peter made him get up. "Stand up," he said, "I am only a man myself." While talking with him, Peter went inside and found a large gathering of people. He said to them: "You are well aware that it is against our law for a Jew to associate with or visit a Gentile. But God has shown me that I should not call anyone impure or unclean. So when I was sent for, I came without raising any objection. May I ask why you sent for me?" Cornelius answered: "Three days ago I was in my house praying at this hour, at three in the afternoon. Suddenly a man in shining clothes stood before me and said, 'Cornelius, God has heard your prayer and remembered your gifts to the poor. Send to Joppa for Simon who is called Peter. He is a guest in the home of Simon the tanner, who lives by the sea.' So I sent for you immediately, and it was good of you to come. Now we are all here in the presence of God to listen to everything the Lord has commanded you to tell us." Then Peter began to speak: "I now realize how true it is that God does not show favoritism but accepts from every nation the one who fears him and does what is right. You know the message God sent to the people of Israel, announcing the good news of peace through Jesus Christ, who is Lord of all. You know what has happened throughout the province of Judea, beginning in Galilee after the baptism that John preached—how God anointed Jesus of Nazareth with the Holy Spirit and power, and how he went around doing good and healing all who were under the power of the devil, because God was with him."

Acts 10:39–48: "We are witnesses of everything he did in the country of the Jews and in Jerusalem. They killed him by hanging him on a cross, but God raised him from the dead on the third day and caused him to be seen. He was not seen by all the people, but by witnesses whom God had already chosen—by us who ate and drank with him after he rose from the dead. He commanded us to preach to the people and to testify that he is the one whom God appointed as judge of the living and the dead. All the prophets testify about him that everyone who believes in him receives forgiveness of sins through his name." While Peter was still speaking these words, the Holy Spirit came on all who heard the message. The circumcised believers who had come with Peter were astonished that the gift of the Holy Spirit had been poured out even on Gentiles. For they heard them speaking in tongues and praising God. Then Peter said, "Surely no one can stand in the way of their being baptized with water. They have received the Holy Spirit just as we have." So he ordered that they be baptized in the name of Jesus Christ. Then they asked Peter to stay with them for a few days. [Note: The Holy Spirit entered into those who accepted Jesus and his forgiveness of sin. It was not till after the Holy Spirit indwelled the new believers that they were baptized with water. This clearly shows that the Holy Spirit indwells at the moment the believer is redeemed by Christ's sacrifice.]

Acts 11:1–14: The apostles and the believers throughout Judea heard that the Gentiles also had received the word of God. So when Peter went up to Jerusalem, the circumcised believers criticized him and said, "You went into the house of uncircumcised men and ate with them." Starting from the beginning, Peter told them the whole story: "I was in the city of Joppa praying, and in a trance I saw a vision. I saw something like a large sheet being let down from heaven by its four corners, and it came down to where I was. I looked into it and saw four-footed animals of the earth, wild beasts, reptiles and birds. Then I heard a voice telling me, 'Get up, Peter. Kill and eat.' I replied, 'Surely not, Lord! Nothing impure or unclean has ever entered my mouth.' The voice spoke from heaven a second time, 'Do not call anything impure that God has made clean.' This happened three times, and then it was all pulled up to heaven again. Right then three men who had been sent to me from Caesarea stopped at the house where I was staying. The Spirit told me to have no hesitation about going with them. These six brothers also went with me, and we entered the man's house. He told us how he had seen an angel appear in his house and say, 'Send to Joppa for Simon who is called Peter. He will bring you a message through which you and all your household will be saved.'"

Acts 11:15–18: "As I began to speak, the Holy Spirit came on them as he had come on us at the beginning. Then I remembered what the Lord had said: 'John baptized with water, but you will be baptized with the Holy Spirit.' So if God gave them the same gift he gave us who believed in the Lord Jesus Christ, who was I to think that I could stand in God's way?" When they heard this, they had no further objections and praised God, saying, "So then, even to Gentiles God has granted repentance that leads to life."

Acts 11:19–24: Now those who had been scattered by the persecution that broke out when Stephen was killed traveled as far as Phoenicia, Cyprus and Antioch, spreading the word only among Jews. Some of them, however, men from Cyprus and Cyrene, went to Antioch and began to speak to Greeks also, telling them the good news about the Lord Jesus. The Lord's hand was with them, and a great number of people believed and turned to the Lord. News of this reached the church in Jerusalem, and they sent Barnabas to Antioch. When he arrived and saw what the grace of God had done, he was glad and encouraged them all to remain true to the Lord with all their hearts. He was a good man, full of the Holy Spirit and faith, and a great number of people were brought to the Lord.

Acts 11:25–30: Then Barnabas went to Tarsus to look for Saul, and when he found him, he brought him to Antioch. So for a whole year Barnabas and Saul met with the church and taught great numbers of people. The disciples were called Christians first at Antioch. During this time some prophets came down from Jerusalem to Antioch. One of them, named Agabus, stood up and through the Spirit predicted that a severe famine would spread over the entire Roman world. (This happened during the reign of Claudius.) The disciples, as each one was able, decided to provide help for the brothers and sisters living in Judea. This they did, sending their gift to the elders by Barnabas and Saul.

Acts 13:1–3: Now in the church at Antioch there were prophets and teachers: Barnabas, Simeon called Niger, Lucius of Cyrene, Manaen (who had been brought up with Herod the tetrarch) and Saul. While they were worshiping the Lord and fasting, the Holy Spirit said, "Set apart for me Barnabas and Saul for the work to which I have called them." So after they had fasted and prayed, they placed their hands on them and sent them off.

Acts 13:4–5: The two of them, sent on their way by the Holy Spirit, went down to Seleucia and sailed from there to Cyprus. When they arrived at Salamis, they proclaimed the word of God in the Jewish synagogues. John was with them as their helper.

Acts 13:6–12: They traveled through the whole island until they came to Paphos. There they met a Jewish sorcerer and false prophet named Bar-Jesus, who was an attendant of the proconsul, Sergius Paulus. The proconsul, an intelligent man, sent for Barnabas and Saul because he wanted to hear the word of God. But Elymas the sorcerer (for that is what his name means) opposed them and tried to turn the proconsul from the faith. Then Saul, who was also called Paul, filled with the Holy Spirit, looked straight at Elymas and said, "You are a child of the devil and an enemy of everything that is right! You are full of all kinds of deceit and trickery. Will you never stop perverting the right ways of the Lord? Now the hand of the Lord is against you. You are going to be blind for a time, not even able to see the light of the sun." Immediately mist and darkness came over him, and he groped about, seeking someone to lead him by the hand. When the proconsul saw what had happened, he believed, for he was amazed at the teaching about the Lord.

Acts 14:1–3: At Iconium Paul and Barnabas went as usual into the Jewish synagogue. There they spoke so effectively that a great number of Jews and Greeks believed. But the Jews who refused to believe stirred up the other Gentiles and poisoned their minds against the brothers. So Paul and Barnabas spent considerable time there, speaking boldly for the Lord, who confirmed the message of his grace by enabling them to perform signs and wonders. [Note: This is one of the places in God's Word where he confirms his inclusion within the Trinity. Jesus promised the Holy Spirit and said he and the Father would live within the redeemed. It is here where you can see affirmation of the Father, Son, and Holy Spirit. Look closely: "… speaking boldly for the Lord, who confirmed the message of his grace by enabling them to perform signs and wonders.")

Acts 15:5–11: Then some of the believers who belonged to the party of the Pharisees stood up and said, "The Gentiles must be circumcised and required to keep the law of Moses." The apostles and elders met to consider this question. After much discussion, Peter got up and addressed them: "Brothers, you know that some time ago God made a choice among you that the Gentiles might hear from my lips the message of the gospel and believe. God, who knows the heart, showed that he accepted them by giving the Holy Spirit to them, just as he did to us. He did not discriminate between us and them, for he purified their hearts by faith. Now then, why do you try to test God by putting on the necks of Gentiles a yoke that neither we nor our ancestors have been able to bear? No! We believe it is through the grace of our Lord Jesus that we are saved, just as they are."

Acts 15:22–29: Then the apostles and elders, with the whole church, decided to choose some of their own men and send them to Antioch with Paul and Barnabas. They chose Judas (called Barsabbas) and Silas, men who were leaders among the believers. With them they sent the following letter: The apostles and elders, your brothers, To the Gentile believers in Antioch, Syria and Cilicia: Greetings. We have heard that some went out from us without our authorization and disturbed you, troubling your minds by what they said. So we all agreed to choose some men and send them to you with our dear friends Barnabas and Paul—men who have risked their lives for the name of our Lord Jesus Christ. Therefore we are sending Judas and Silas to confirm by word of mouth what we are writing. It seemed good to the Holy Spirit and to us not to burden you with anything beyond the following requirements: You are to abstain from food sacrificed to idols, from blood, from the meat of strangled animals and from sexual immorality. You will do well to avoid these things. Farewell.

Acts 16:6–10: Paul and his companions traveled throughout the region of Phrygia and Galatia, having been kept by the Holy Spirit from preaching the word in the province of Asia. When they came to the border of Mysia, they tried to enter Bithynia, but the Spirit of Jesus would not allow them to. So they passed by Mysia and went down to Troas. During the night Paul had a vision of a man of Macedonia standing and begging him, "Come over to Macedonia and help us." After Paul had seen the vision, we got ready at once to leave for Macedonia, concluding that God had called us to preach the gospel to them. [Note: The Holy Spirit not only indwells, fills, inspires, enlightens, sets apart, and guides, but he also restrains according to the will of the Father.]

Acts 19:1–7: While Apollos was at Corinth, Paul took the road through the interior and arrived at Ephesus. There he found some disciples and asked them, "Did you receive the Holy Spirit when you believed?" They answered, "No, we have not even heard that there is a Holy Spirit." So Paul asked, "Then what baptism did you receive?" "John's baptism," they replied. Paul said, "John's baptism was a baptism of repentance. He told the people to believe in the one coming after him, that is, in Jesus." On hearing this, they were baptized in the name of the Lord Jesus. When Paul placed his hands on them, the Holy Spirit came on them, and they spoke in tongues and prophesied. There were about twelve men in all. [Note: This is another area where confusion arises. The scripture states that Paul laid hands on the disciples after they were water baptized. When the Holy Spirit "came on them ... they spoke in tongues and prophesied." The Holy Spirit had already entered into the disciples when they accepted Paul's message of Jesus. It was the Holy Spirit using Paul as his instrument of affirmation where he enabled the redeemed disciples to speak in tongues and prophecy. It was no power displayed by Paul. The permanently indwelled by the Holy

Spirit can immediately respond to his filling even in the moment of receiving the salvation of Jesus.]

Acts 20:13–24: We went on ahead to the ship and sailed for Assos, where we were going to take Paul aboard. He had made this arrangement because he was going there on foot. When he met us at Assos, we took him aboard and went on to Mitylene. The next day we set sail from there and arrived off Chios. The day after that we crossed over to Samos, and on the following day arrived at Miletus. Paul had decided to sail past Ephesus to avoid spending time in the province of Asia, for he was in a hurry to reach Jerusalem, if possible, by the day of Pentecost. From Miletus, Paul sent to Ephesus for the elders of the church. When they arrived, he said to them: "You know how I lived the whole time I was with you, from the first day I came into the province of Asia. I served the Lord with great humility and with tears and in the midst of severe testing by the plots of my Jewish opponents. You know that I have not hesitated to preach anything that would be helpful to you but have taught you publicly and from house to house. I have declared to both Jews and Greeks that they must turn to God in repentance and have faith in our Lord Jesus. And now, compelled by the Spirit, I am going to Jerusalem, not knowing what will happen to me there. I only know that in every city the Holy Spirit warns me that prison and hardships are facing me. However, I consider my life worth nothing to me; my only aim is to finish the race and complete the task the Lord Jesus has given me—the task of testifying to the good news of God's grace."

Acts 20:25–28: Now I know that none of you among whom I have gone about preaching the kingdom will ever see me again. Therefore, I declare to you today that I am innocent of the blood of any of you. For I have not hesitated to proclaim to you the whole will of God. Keep watch over yourselves and all the flock of which the Holy Spirit has made you overseers. Be shepherds of the church of God, which he bought with his own blood.

Acts 21:1–6: After we had torn ourselves away from them, we put out to sea and sailed straight to Kos. The next day we went to Rhodes and from there to Patara. We found a ship crossing over to Phoenicia, went on board and set sail. After sighting Cyprus and passing to the south of it, we sailed on to Syria. We landed at Tyre, where our ship was to unload its cargo. We sought out the disciples there and stayed with them seven days. Through the Spirit they urged Paul not to go on to Jerusalem. When it was time to leave, we left and continued on our way. All of them, including wives and children, accompanied us out of the city, and there on the beach we knelt to pray. After saying good-bye to each other, we went aboard the ship, and they returned home.

Acts 21:7–11: We continued our voyage from Tyre and landed at Ptolemais, where we greeted the brothers and sisters and stayed with them for a day. Leaving the next day, we reached Caesarea and stayed at the house of Philip the evangelist, one of the Seven. He had four unmarried daughters who prophesied. After we had been there a number of days, a prophet named Agabus came down from Judea. Coming over to us, he took Paul's belt, tied his own hands and feet with it and said, "The Holy Spirit says, 'In this way the Jewish leaders in Jerusalem will bind the owner of this belt and will hand him over to the Gentiles.'"

Acts 23:9–11: There was a great uproar, and some of the teachers of the law who were Pharisees stood up and argued vigorously. "We find nothing wrong with this man," they said. "What if a spirit or an angel has spoken to him?" The dispute became so violent that the commander was afraid Paul would be torn to pieces by them. He ordered the troops to go down and take him away from them by force and bring him into the barracks. The following night the Lord stood near Paul and said, "Take courage! As you have testified about me in Jerusalem, so you must also testify in Rome." [Note: The following night, the Lord stood near Paul and said, "Take courage!" The Holy Spirit was surely present in the person of Jesus, the Lord.]

Acts 28:17–28: Three days later he called together the local Jewish leaders. When they had assembled, Paul said to them: "My brothers, although I have done nothing against our people or against the customs of our ancestors, I was arrested in Jerusalem and handed over to the Romans. They examined me and wanted to release me, because I was not guilty of any crime deserving death. The Jews objected, so I was compelled to make an appeal to Caesar. I certainly did not intend to bring any charge against my own people. For this reason I have asked to see you and talk with you. It is because of the hope of Israel that I am bound with this chain." They replied, "We have not received any letters from Judea concerning you, and none of our people who have come from there has reported or said anything bad about you. But we want to hear what your views are, for we know that people everywhere are talking against this sect." They arranged to meet Paul on a certain day, and came in even larger numbers to the place where he was staying. He witnessed to them from morning till evening, explaining about the kingdom of God, and from the Law of Moses and from the Prophets he tried to persuade them about Jesus. Some were convinced by what he said, but others would not believe. They disagreed among themselves and began to leave after Paul had made this final statement: "The Holy Spirit spoke the truth to your ancestors when he said through Isaiah the prophet: 'Go to this people and say, "You will be ever hearing but never understanding; you will be ever seeing but never perceiving." For this people's heart has become calloused; they hardly hear with their ears, and they have closed their eyes. Otherwise they might see with their eyes, hear with their ears, understand with their hearts and turn, and I would heal them.' Therefore I want you to know that God's salvation has been sent to the Gentiles, and they will listen!"

Romans 1:2–4: The gospel he promised beforehand through his prophets in the Holy Scriptures regarding his Son, who as to his earthly life was a descendant of David, and who through the Spirit of holiness was appointed the Son of God in power by his resurrection from the dead: Jesus Christ our Lord.

Romans 2:28–29: A person is not a Jew who is one only outwardly, nor is circumcision merely outward and physical. No, a person is a Jew who is one inwardly; and circumcision is circumcision of the heart, by the Spirit, not by the written code. Such a person's praise is not from other people, but from God.

Romans 5:5–8: And hope does not put us to shame, because God's love has been poured out into our hearts through the Holy Spirit, who has been given to us. You see, at just the right time, when we were still powerless, Christ died for the ungodly. Very rarely will anyone die for a righteous person, though for a good person someone might possibly dare to die. But God demonstrates his own love for us in this: While we were still sinners, Christ died for us.

Romans 7:4–6: So, my brothers and sisters, you also died to the law through the body of Christ, that you might belong to another, to him who was raised from the dead, in order that we might bear fruit for God. For when we were in the realm of the flesh, the sinful passions aroused by the law were at work in us, so that we bore fruit for death. But now, by dying to what once bound us, we have been released from the law so that we serve in the new way of the Spirit, and not in the old way of the written code.

Romans 8:1–4: Therefore, there is now no condemnation for those who are in Christ Jesus, because through Christ Jesus the law of the Spirit who gives life has set you free from the law of sin and death. For what the law was powerless to do because it was weakened by the flesh, God did by sending his own Son in the likeness of sinful flesh to be a sin offering. And so he condemned sin in the flesh, in order that the righteous requirement of the law might be fully met in us, who do not live according to the flesh but according to the Spirit.

Romans 8:5–11: Those who live according to the flesh have their minds set on what the flesh desires; but those who live in accordance with the Spirit have their minds set on what the Spirit desires. The mind governed by the flesh is death, but the mind governed by the

Spirit is life and peace. The mind governed by the flesh is hostile to God; it does not submit to God's law, nor can it do so. Those who are in the realm of the flesh cannot please God. You, however, are not in the realm of the flesh but are in the realm of the Spirit, if indeed the Spirit of God lives in you. And if anyone does not have the Spirit of Christ, they do not belong to Christ. But if Christ is in you, then even though your body is subject to death because of sin, the Spirit gives life because of righteousness. And if the Spirit of him who raised Jesus from the dead is living in you, he who raised Christ from the dead will also give life to your mortal bodies because of his Spirit who lives in you.

Romans 8:12–17: Therefore, brothers and sisters, we have an obligation—but it is not to the flesh, to live according to it. For if you live according to the flesh, you will die; but if by the Spirit you put to death the misdeeds of the body, you will live. For those who are led by the Spirit of God are the children of God. The Spirit you received does not make you slaves, so that you live in fear again; rather, the Spirit you received brought about your adoption to sonship. And by him we cry, *"Abba,* Father." The Spirit himself testifies with our spirit that we are God's children. Now if we are children, then we are heirs—heirs of God and co-heirs with Christ, if indeed we share in his sufferings in order that we may also share in his glory.

Romans 8:22–25: We know that the whole creation has been groaning as in the pains of childbirth right up to the present time. Not only so, but we ourselves, who have the firstfruits of the Spirit, groan inwardly as we wait eagerly for our adoption to sonship, the redemption of our bodies. For in this hope we were saved. But hope that is seen is no hope at all. Who hopes for what they already have? But if we hope for what we do not yet have, we wait for it patiently.

Romans 8:26–28: In the same way, the Spirit helps us in our weakness. We do not know what we ought to pray for, but the Spirit himself intercedes for us through wordless groans. And he who searches our hearts knows the mind of the Spirit, because the Spirit intercedes for God's people in accordance with the will of God. And we know that in all things God works for the good of those who love him, who have been called according to his purpose.

Romans 9:1–5: I speak the truth in Christ—I am not lying, my conscience confirms it through the Holy Spirit—I have great sorrow and unceasing anguish in my heart. For I could wish that I myself were cursed and cut off from Christ for the sake of my people, those of my own race, the people of Israel. Theirs is the adoption to sonship; theirs the divine glory, the covenants, the receiving of the law, the temple worship and the promises. Theirs are the patriarchs, and from them is traced the human ancestry of the Messiah, who is God over all, forever praised! Amen.

Romans: 14:17–19: For the kingdom of God is not a matter of eating and drinking, but of righteousness, peace and joy in the Holy Spirit, because anyone who serves Christ in this way is pleasing to God and receives human approval. Let us therefore make every effort to do what leads to peace and to mutual edification.

Romans 15:13: May the God of hope fill you with all joy and peace as you trust in him, so that you may overflow with hope by the power of the Holy Spirit.

Romans 15: 15–16: Yet I have written you quite boldly on some points to remind you of them again, because of the grace God gave me to be a minister of Christ Jesus to the Gentiles. He gave me the priestly duty of proclaiming the gospel of God, so that the Gentiles might become an offering acceptable to God, sanctified by the Holy Spirit.

Romans 15:17–19: Therefore I glory in Christ Jesus in my service to God. I will not venture to speak of anything except what Christ has accomplished through me in leading the Gentiles to obey God by what I have said and done— by the power of signs and wonders, through the power of the Spirit of God. So from Jerusalem all the way around to Illyricum, I have fully proclaimed the gospel of Christ.

Romans 15:30: I urge you, brothers and sisters, by our Lord Jesus Christ and by the love of the Spirit, to join me in my struggle by praying to God for me.

1 Corinthians 2:1–5: And so it was with me, brothers and sisters. When I came to you, I did not come with eloquence or human wisdom as I proclaimed to you the testimony about God. For I resolved to know nothing while I was with you except Jesus Christ and him crucified. I came to you in weakness with great fear and trembling. My message and my preaching were not with wise and persuasive words, but with a demonstration of the Spirit's power, so that your faith might not rest on human wisdom, but on God's power.

1 Corinthians 2:6–10: We do, however, speak a message of wisdom among the mature, but not the wisdom of this age or of the rulers of this age, who are coming to nothing. No, we declare God's wisdom, a mystery that has been hidden and that God destined for our glory before time began. None of the rulers of this age understood it, for if they had, they would not have crucified the Lord of glory. However, as it is written: "What no eye has seen, what no ear has heard, and what no human mind has conceived"—the things God has prepared for those who love him—these are the things God has revealed to us by his Spirit. The Spirit searches all things, even the deep things of God.

1 Corinthians 2:11–16: For who knows a person's thoughts except their own spirit within them? In the same way no one knows the thoughts of God except the Spirit of God. What we have received is not the spirit of the world, but the Spirit who is from God, so that we may understand what God has freely given us. This is what we speak, not in words taught us by human wisdom but in words taught by the Spirit, explaining spiritual realities with Spirit-taught words. The person without the Spirit does not accept the things that come from the Spirit of God but considers them foolishness, and cannot understand them because they are discerned only through the

Spirit. The person with the Spirit makes judgments about all things, but such a person is not subject to merely human judgments, for, "Who has known the mind of the Lord so as to instruct him?" But we have the mind of Christ.

1 Corinthians 3:16–23: Don't you know that you yourselves are God's temple and that God's Spirit dwells in your midst? If anyone destroys God's temple, God will destroy that person; for God's temple is sacred, and you together are that temple. Do not deceive yourselves. If any of you think you are wise by the standards of this age, you should become "fools" so that you may become wise. For the wisdom of this world is foolishness in God's sight. As it is written: "He catches the wise in their craftiness"; and again, "The Lord knows that the thoughts of the wise are futile." So then, no more boasting about human leaders! All things are yours, whether Paul or Apollos or Cephas or the world or life or death or the present or the future—all are yours, and you are of Christ, and Christ is of God.

1 Corinthians 6:9–11: Or do you not know that wrongdoers will not inherit the kingdom of God? Do not be deceived: Neither the sexually immoral nor idolaters nor adulterers nor men who have sex with men nor thieves nor the greedy nor drunkards nor slanderers nor swindlers will inherit the kingdom of God. And that is what some of you were. But you were washed, you were sanctified, you were justified in the name of the Lord Jesus Christ and by the Spirit of our God.

1 Corinthians 6:17–20: But whoever is united with the Lord is one with him in spirit. Flee from sexual immorality. All other sins a person commits are outside the body, but whoever sins sexually, sins against their own body. Do you not know that your bodies are temples of the Holy Spirit, who is in you, whom you have received from God? You are not your own; you were bought at a price. Therefore honor God with your bodies.

1 Corinthians 7:40: … and I think that I too have the Spirit of God.

1 Corinthians 12:1–3: Now about the gifts of the Spirit, brothers and sisters, I do not want you to be uninformed. You know that when you were pagans, somehow or other you were influenced and led astray to mute idols. Therefore I want you to know that no one who is speaking by the Spirit of God says, "Jesus be cursed," and no one can say, "Jesus is Lord," except by the Holy Spirit. [Note: This confirms that each and every redeemed believer is indwelled by the Holy Spirit. There is no waiting period or special experience, after salvation, needed to receive the Holy Spirit.]

1 Corinthians 12:4–6: There are different kinds of gifts, but the same Spirit distributes them. There are different kinds of service, but the same Lord. There are different kinds of working, but in all of them and in everyone it is the same God at work. [Note: The word "same" plainly and clearly means "one and the same"—the Three in One at work in complete unison.]

1 Corinthians 12:7–11: Now to each one the manifestation of the Spirit is given for the common good. To one there is given through the Spirit a message of wisdom, to another a message of knowledge by means of the same Spirit, to another faith by the same Spirit, to another gifts of healing by that one Spirit, to another miraculous powers, to another prophecy, to another distinguishing between spirits, to another speaking in different kinds of tongues, and to still another the interpretation of tongues. All these are the work of one and the same Spirit, and he distributes them to each one, just as he determines. [Note: The Holy Spirit, already indwelling each and every redeemed believer, through his manifestation given for the common good, gives each one according to his determination. These manifestations are not personally selective; nor are they to be touted as exclusive by any brother or sister in Christ.]

1 Corinthians 12:12–13: Just as a body, though one, has many parts, but all its many parts form one body, so it is with Christ. For we were all baptized by one Spirit so as to form one body— whether Jews or Gentiles, slave or free—and we were all given the one Spirit to drink. [Note: The "many parts" represent the complete body of Christ—the church. We are *all* indwelled and empowered by the Holy Spirit from the moment of salvation. This is the absolute meaning of "all baptized by one Spirit so as to form one body." Thus, this once again confirms God's plan ("For God so loved the world, that He gave His only begotten Son, that whosoever believeth in Him should not perish, but have everlasting life." [KJV]) The "whosoever" encompasses and fully includes each and every redeemed soul, as is promised. Through the will and love of the Father and the unconditional sacrifice of the Son, Jesus, the Holy Spirit—the one Spirit we were all given to drink—enters the redeemed at the instant of salvation, permanently baptizing with power and bestowing forever everlasting life.]

2 Corinthians 1:21–22: Now it is God who makes both us and you stand firm in Christ. He anointed us, set his seal of ownership on us, and put his Spirit in our hearts as a deposit, guaranteeing what is to come.

2 Corinthians 3:1–3: Are we beginning to commend ourselves again? Or do we need, like some people, letters of recommendation to you or from you? You yourselves are our letter, written on our hearts, known and read by everyone. You show that you are a letter from Christ, the result of our ministry, written not with ink but with the Spirit of the living God, not on tablets of stone but on tablets of human hearts.

2 Corinthians 3:4–6: Such confidence we have through Christ before God. Not that we are competent in ourselves to claim anything for ourselves, but our competence comes from God. He has made us competent as ministers of a new covenant—not of the letter but of the Spirit; for the letter kills, but the Spirit gives life.

2 Corinthians 3:7–12: Now if the ministry that brought death, which was engraved in letters on stone, came with glory, so that the Israelites could not look steadily at the face of Moses because of its glory, transitory though it was, will not the ministry of the Spirit be even more glorious? If the ministry that brought condemnation was glorious, how much more glorious is the ministry that brings righteousness! For what was glorious has no glory now in comparison with the surpassing glory. And if what was transitory came with glory, how much greater is the glory of that which lasts! Therefore, since we have such a hope, we are very bold.

2 Corinthians 3:13–18: We are not like Moses, who would put a veil over his face to prevent the Israelites from seeing the end of what was passing away. But their minds were made dull, for to this day the same veil remains when the old covenant is read. It has not been removed, because only in Christ is it taken away. Even to this day when Moses is read, a veil covers their hearts. But whenever anyone turns to the Lord, the veil is taken away. Now the Lord is the Spirit, and where the Spirit of the Lord is, there is freedom. And we all, who with unveiled faces contemplate the Lord's glory, are being transformed into his image with ever-increasing glory, which comes from the Lord, who is the Spirit.

2 Corinthians 5:1–6: For we know that if the earthly tent we live in is destroyed, we have a building from God, an eternal house in heaven, not built by human hands. Meanwhile we groan, longing to be clothed instead with our heavenly dwelling, because when we are clothed, we will not be found naked. For while we are in this tent, we groan and are burdened, because we do not wish to be unclothed but to be clothed instead with our heavenly dwelling, so that what is mortal may be swallowed up by life. Now the one who has fashioned us for this very purpose is God, who has given us the Spirit as a deposit, guaranteeing what is to come. Therefore we are always confident and know that as long as we are at home in the body we are away from the Lord.

2 Corinthians 6:3–10: We put no stumbling block in anyone's path, so that our ministry will not be discredited. Rather, as servants of God we commend ourselves in every way: in great endurance; in troubles, hardships and distresses; in beatings, imprisonments and riots; in hard work, sleepless nights and hunger; in purity, understanding, patience and kindness; in the Holy Spirit and in sincere love; in truthful speech and in the power of God; with weapons of righteousness in the right hand and in the left; through glory and dishonor, bad report and good report; genuine, yet regarded as impostors; known, yet regarded as unknown; dying, and yet we live on; beaten, and yet not killed; sorrowful, yet always rejoicing; poor, yet making many rich; having nothing, and yet possessing everything.

2 Corinthians 13:14: May the grace of the Lord Jesus Christ, and the love of God, and the fellowship of the Holy Spirit be with you all. [Note: See here the complete Holy Trinity working as one and blessing as one.]

Galatians 3:1–5: You foolish Galatians! Who has bewitched you? Before your very eyes Jesus Christ was clearly portrayed as crucified. I would like to learn just one thing from you: Did you receive the Spirit by the works of the law, or by believing what you heard? Are you so foolish? After beginning by means of the Spirit, are you now trying to finish by means of the flesh? Have you experienced so much in vain—if it really was in vain? So again I ask, does God give you his Spirit and work miracles among you by the works of the law, or by your believing what you heard?

Galatians 3:10–14: For all who rely on the works of the law are under a curse, as it is written: "Cursed is everyone who does not continue to do everything written in the Book of the Law." Clearly no one who relies on the law is justified before God, because "the righteous will live by faith." The law is not based on faith; on the contrary, it says, "The person who does these things will live by them." Christ redeemed us from the curse of the law by becoming a curse for us, for it is written: "Cursed is everyone who is hung on a pole." He redeemed us in order that the blessing given to Abraham might come to the Gentiles through Christ Jesus, so that by faith we might receive the promise of the Spirit.

Galatians 3:26–29: So in Christ Jesus you are all children of God through faith, for all of you who were baptized into Christ have clothed yourselves with Christ. There is neither Jew nor Gentile, neither slave nor free, nor is there male and female, for you are all one in Christ Jesus. If you belong to Christ, then you are Abraham's seed, and heirs according to the promise.

Galatians 4:1–7: What I am saying is that as long as an heir is underage, he is no different from a slave, although he owns the whole estate. The heir is subject to guardians and trustees until the time set by his father. So also, when we were underage, we were in slavery under the elemental spiritual forces of the world. But when the set time had fully come, God sent his Son, born of a woman, born under the law, to redeem those under the law, that we might receive adoption to sonship. Because you are his sons, God sent the Spirit of his Son into our hearts, the Spirit who calls out, *"Abba*, Father." So you are no longer a slave, but God's child; and since you are his child, God has made you also an heir. [Note: This passage presents the confirmation of the universality of our place with Christ as his redeemed; whether Jew or Gentile, we are all equally indwelled by the Holy Spirit, and *you are his child; God has made you also an heir.* No other avenue exists to be indwelled by the Holy Spirit promised by the Lord, Jesus Christ.]

Galatians 4:28–29: Now you, brothers and sisters, like Isaac, are children of promise. At that time the son born according to the flesh persecuted the son born by the power of the Spirit. It is the same now.

Galatians 5:5–6: For through the Spirit we eagerly await by faith the righteousness for which we hope. For in Christ Jesus neither circumcision nor uncircumcision has any value. The only thing that counts is faith expressing itself through love. [Note: This truth also points to the fact that exclusivity is not a part of God's universal plan of the indwelling Holy Spirit. There is one Spirit and one baptism of the Spirit. No special anointing of the Holy Spirit is required after salvation. The Holy Spirit will enable—fill—as he determines is useful for the common good and to God's glory.]

Galatians 5:16–18: So I say, walk by the Spirit, and you will not gratify the desires of the flesh. For the flesh desires what is contrary to the Spirit, and the Spirit what is contrary to the flesh. They are in conflict with each other, so that you are not to do whatever you want. But if you are led by the Spirit, you are not under the law.

Galatians 5:22–26: But the fruit of the Spirit is love, joy, peace, patience, kindness, goodness, faithfulness, gentleness, and self-control. Against such things there is no law. Those who belong to Christ Jesus have crucified the flesh with its passions and desires. Since we live by the Spirit, let us keep in step with the Spirit. Let us not become conceited, provoking and envying each other. [Note: Since we live by the Spirit, let us keep in step with the Spirit.]

Galatians 6:6–10: Nevertheless, the one who receives instruction in the word should share all good things with their instructor. Do not be deceived: God cannot be mocked. A man reaps what he sows. Whoever sows to please their flesh, from the flesh will reap destruction; whoever sows to please the Spirit, from the Spirit will reap eternal life. Let us not become weary in doing good, for at the proper time we will reap a harvest if we do not give up. Therefore, as we have opportunity, let us do good to all people, especially to those who belong to the family of believers.

Ephesians 1:13–14: And you also were included in Christ when you heard the message of truth, the gospel of your salvation. When you believed, you were marked in him with a seal, the promised Holy Spirit, who is a deposit guaranteeing our inheritance until the redemption of those who are God's possession—to the praise of his glory.

Ephesians 1:17: I keep asking that the God of our Lord Jesus Christ, the glorious Father, may give you the Spirit of wisdom and revelation, so that you may know him better.

Ephesians 2:13–22: But now in Christ Jesus you who once were far away have been brought near by the blood of Christ. For he himself is our peace, who has made the two groups one and has destroyed the barrier, the dividing wall of hostility, by setting aside in his flesh the law with its commands and regulations. His purpose was to create in himself one new humanity out of the two, thus making peace, and in one body to reconcile both of them to God through the cross, by which he put to death their hostility. He came and preached peace to you who were far away and peace to those who were near. For through him we both have access to the Father by one Spirit. Consequently, you are no longer foreigners and strangers, but fellow citizens with God's people and also members of his household, built on the foundation of the apostles and prophets, with Christ Jesus himself as the chief cornerstone. In him the whole building is joined together and rises to become a holy temple in the Lord. And in him you too are being built together to become a dwelling in which God lives by his Spirit.

Ephesians 3:2–6: Surely you have heard about the administration of God's grace that was given to me for you, that is, the mystery made known to me by revelation, as I have already written briefly. In reading this, then, you will be able to understand my insight into the mystery of Christ, which was not made known to people in other generations as it has now been revealed by the Spirit to God's holy apostles and prophets. This mystery is that through the gospel the Gentiles are heirs together with Israel, members together of one body, and sharers together in the promise in Christ Jesus.

Ephesians 3:14–21: For this reason I kneel before the Father, from whom every family in heaven and on earth derives its name. I pray that out of his glorious riches he may strengthen you with power through his Spirit in your inner being, so that Christ may dwell in your hearts through faith. And I pray that you, being rooted and established in love, may have power, together with all the Lord's holy people, to grasp how wide and long and high and deep is the love of Christ, and to know this love that surpasses knowledge—that you may be filled to the measure of all the fullness of God. Now to him who is able to do immeasurably more than all we ask or imagine, according to his power that is at work within us, to him be glory in the church and in Christ Jesus throughout all generations, for ever and ever! Amen.

Ephesians 4:1–6: As a prisoner for the Lord, then, I urge you to live a life worthy of the calling you have received. Be completely humble and gentle; be patient, bearing with one another in love. Make every effort to keep the unity of the Spirit through the bond of peace. There is one body and one Spirit, just as you were called to one hope when you were called; one Lord, one faith, one baptism; one God and Father of all, who is over all and through all and in all.

Ephesians 4:15–32: Instead, speaking the truth in love, we will grow to become in every respect the mature body of him who is the head, that is, Christ. From him the whole body, joined and held together by every supporting ligament, grows and builds itself up in love, as each part does its work. So I tell you this, and insist on it in the Lord, that you must no longer live as the Gentiles do, in the futility of their thinking. They are darkened in their understanding and separated from the life of God because of the ignorance that is in them due to the hardening of their hearts. Having lost all sensitivity, they have given themselves over to sensuality so as to indulge in every kind of impurity, and they are full of greed. That, however, is not the way of life you learned when you heard about Christ and were taught in him in accordance with the truth that is in Jesus. You were taught, with regard to your former way of life, to put off your old self, which is being corrupted by its deceitful desires; to be made new in the attitude of your minds; and to put on the new self, created to be like God in true righteousness and holiness. Therefore each of you must put off falsehood and speak truthfully to your neighbor, for we are all members of one body. "In your anger do not sin": Do not let the sun go down while you are still angry, and do not give the devil a foothold. Anyone who has been stealing must steal no longer, but must work, doing something useful with their own hands, that they may have something to share with those in need. Do not let any unwholesome talk come out of your mouths, but only what is helpful for building others up according to their needs, that it may benefit those who listen. And do not grieve the Holy Spirit of God, with whom you were sealed for the day of redemption. Get rid of all bitterness, rage and anger, brawling and slander, along with every form of malice. Be kind and compassionate to one another, forgiving each other, just as in Christ God forgave you.

Ephesians 5:8–21: For you were once darkness, but now you are light in the Lord. Live as children of light (for the fruit of the light consists in all goodness, righteousness and truth) and find out what pleases the Lord. Have nothing to do with the fruitless deeds of darkness, but rather expose them. It is shameful even to mention what the disobedient do in secret. But everything exposed by the light becomes visible—and everything that is illuminated becomes a light. This is why it is said: "Wake up, sleeper, rise from the dead, and Christ will shine on you." Be very careful, then, how you live—not as unwise but as wise, making the most of every opportunity, because the days are evil. Therefore do not be foolish, but understand what the Lord's will is. Do not get drunk on wine, which leads to debauchery. Instead, be filled with the Spirit, speaking to one another with psalms, hymns, and songs from the Spirit. Sing and make music from your heart to the Lord, always giving thanks to God the Father for everything, in the name of our Lord Jesus Christ. Submit to one another out of reverence for Christ.

Ephesians 6:10–18: Finally, be strong in the Lord and in his mighty power. Put on the full armor of God, so that you can take your stand against the devil's schemes. For our struggle is not against flesh and blood, but against the rulers, against the authorities, against the powers of this dark world and against the spiritual forces of evil in the heavenly realms. Therefore put on the full armor of God, so that when the day of evil comes, you may be able to stand your ground, and after you have done everything, to stand. Stand firm then, with the belt of truth buckled around your waist, with the breastplate of righteousness in place, and with your feet fitted with the readiness that comes from the gospel of peace. In addition to all this, take up the shield of faith, with which you can extinguish all the flaming arrows of the evil one. Take the helmet of salvation and the sword of the Spirit, which is the word of God. And pray in the Spirit on all occasions with all kinds of prayers and requests. With this in mind, be alert and always keep on praying for all the Lord's people.

Philippians 1:15−21: It is true that some preach Christ out of envy and rivalry, but others out of goodwill. The latter do so out of love, knowing that I am put here for the defense of the gospel. The former preach Christ out of selfish ambition, not sincerely, supposing that they can stir up trouble for me while I am in chains. But what does it matter? The important thing is that in every way, whether from false motives or true, Christ is preached. And because of this I rejoice. Yes, and I will continue to rejoice, for I know that through your prayers and God's provision of the Spirit of Jesus Christ what has happened to me will turn out for my deliverance. I eagerly expect and hope that I will in no way be ashamed, but will have sufficient courage so that now as always Christ will be exalted in my body, whether by life or by death. For to me, to live is Christ and to die is gain.

Philippians 2:1−5: Therefore if you have any encouragement from being united with Christ, if any comfort from his love, if any common sharing in the Spirit, if any tenderness and compassion, then make my joy complete by being like-minded, having the same love, being one in spirit and of one mind. Do nothing out of selfish ambition or vain conceit. Rather, in humility value others above yourselves, not looking to your own interests but each of you to the interests of the others. In your relationships with one another, have the same mindset as Christ Jesus.

Philippians 3:1−4: Further, my brothers and sisters, rejoice in the Lord! It is no trouble for me to write the same things to you again, and it is a safeguard for you. Watch out for those dogs, those evildoers, those mutilators of the flesh. For it is we who are the circumcision, we who serve God by his Spirit, who boast in Christ Jesus, and who put no confidence in the flesh—though I myself have reasons for such confidence. If someone else thinks they have reasons to put confidence in the flesh, I have more.

Colossians 1:3–8: We always thank God, the Father of our Lord Jesus Christ, when we pray for you, because we have heard of your faith in Christ Jesus and of the love you have for all God's people— the faith and love that spring from the hope stored up for you in heaven and about which you have already heard in the true message of the gospel that has come to you. In the same way, the gospel is bearing fruit and growing throughout the whole world—just as it has been doing among you since the day you heard it and truly understood God's grace. You learned it from Epaphras, our dear fellow servant, who is a faithful minister of Christ on our behalf, and who also told us of your love in the Spirit.

1 Thessalonians 1:1–10: Paul, Silas and Timothy, To the church of the Thessalonians in God the Father and the Lord Jesus Christ: Grace and peace to you. We always thank God for all of you and continually mention you in our prayers. We remember before our God and Father your work produced by faith, your labor prompted by love, and your endurance inspired by hope in our Lord Jesus Christ. For we know, brothers and sisters loved by God, that he has chosen you, because our gospel came to you not simply with words but also with power, with the Holy Spirit and deep conviction. You know how we lived among you for your sake. You became imitators of us and of the Lord, for you welcomed the message in the midst of severe suffering with the joy given by the Holy Spirit. And so you became a model to all the believers in Macedonia and Achaia. The Lord's message rang out from you not only in Macedonia and Achaia—your faith in God has become known everywhere. Therefore we do not need to say anything about it, for they themselves report what kind of reception you gave us. They tell how you turned to God from idols to serve the living and true God, and to wait for his Son from heaven, whom he raised from the dead—Jesus, who rescues us from the coming wrath.

1 Thessalonians 4:2–8: For you know what instructions we gave you by the authority of the Lord Jesus. It is God's will that you should be sanctified: that you should avoid sexual immorality; that each of you should learn to control your own body in a way that is holy and honorable, not in passionate lust like the pagans, who do not know God; and that in this matter no one should wrong or take advantage of a brother or sister. The Lord will punish all those who commit such sins, as we told you and warned you before. For God did not call us to be impure, but to live a holy life. Therefore, anyone who rejects this instruction does not reject a human being but God, the very God who gives you his Holy Spirit.

1 Thessalonians 5:16–24: Rejoice always, pray continually, give thanks in all circumstances; for this is God's will for you in Christ Jesus. Do not quench the Spirit. Do not treat prophecies with contempt but test them all; hold on to what is good, reject every kind of evil. May God himself, the God of peace, sanctify you through and through. May your whole spirit, soul and body be kept blameless at the coming of our Lord Jesus Christ. The one who calls you is faithful, and he will do it.

2 Thessalonians 2:7: For the secret power of lawlessness is already at work; but the one who now holds it back will continue to do so till he is taken out of the way. [Note: "The one who now holds it back" is the Holy Spirit.]

2 Thessalonians 2:13–17: But we ought always to thank God for you, brothers and sisters loved by the Lord, because God chose you as firstfruits to be saved through the sanctifying work of the Spirit and through belief in the truth. He called you to this through our gospel, that you might share in the glory of our Lord Jesus Christ. So then, brothers and sisters, stand firm and hold fast to the teachings we passed on to you, whether by word of mouth or by letter. May our

Lord Jesus Christ himself and God our Father, who loved us and by his grace gave us eternal encouragement and good hope, encourage your hearts and strengthen you in every good deed and word.

1 Timothy 3:16: Beyond all question, the mystery from which true godliness springs is great: He appeared in the flesh, was vindicated by the Spirit, was seen by angels, was preached among the nations, was believed on in the world, was taken up in glory.

1 Timothy 4:1–5: The Spirit clearly says that in later times some will abandon the faith and follow deceiving spirits and things taught by demons. Such teachings come through hypocritical liars, whose consciences have been seared as with a hot iron. They forbid people to marry and order them to abstain from certain foods, which God created to be received with thanksgiving by those who believe and who know the truth. For everything God created is good, and nothing is to be rejected if it is received with thanksgiving, because it is consecrated by the word of God and prayer.

2 Timothy 1:7: For the Spirit God gave us does not make us timid, but gives us power, love and self-discipline. [Note: Here is yet another affirmation of God's gift to each of his, the redeemed. With his salvation freely given through the ultimate sacrifice of Jesus on the cross, it is the blessed universal gift of God—The Holy Spirit—that empowers each saved one. It would be impossible to live the Christian life without his constant power, love and self-discipline.]

2 Timothy 1: 13–14: What you heard from me, keep as the pattern of sound teaching, with faith and love in Christ Jesus. Guard the good deposit that was entrusted to you—guard it with the help of the Holy Spirit who lives in us.

Titus 3:3–8: At one time we too were foolish, disobedient, deceived and enslaved by all kinds of passions and pleasures. We lived in malice and envy, being hated and hating one another. But when the kindness and love of God our Savior appeared, he saved us, not because of righteous things we had done, but because of his mercy. He saved us through the washing of rebirth and renewal by the Holy Spirit, whom he poured out on us generously through Jesus Christ our Savior, so that, having been justified by his grace, we might become heirs having the hope of eternal life. This is a trustworthy saying. And I want you to stress these things, so that those who have trusted in God may be careful to devote themselves to doing what is good. These things are excellent and profitable for everyone. [Note: Take a very close look at the plan of the Father, Son, and Holy Spirit working in complete unison. This continues today and beyond.]

Hebrews 2:1–4: We must pay the most careful attention, therefore, to what we have heard, so that we do not drift away. For since the message spoken through angels was binding, and every violation and disobedience received its just punishment, how shall we escape if we ignore so great a salvation? This salvation, which was first announced by the Lord, was confirmed to us by those who heard him. God also testified to it by signs, wonders and various miracles, and by gifts of the Holy Spirit distributed according to his will.

Hebrews 3:7–15, 19: So, as the Holy Spirit says: "Today, if you hear his voice, do not harden your hearts as you did in the rebellion, during the time of testing in the wilderness, where your ancestors tested and tried me, though for forty years they saw what I did. That is why I was angry with that generation; I said, 'Their hearts are always going astray, and they have not known my ways.' So I declared on oath in my anger, 'They shall never enter my rest.'" See to it, brothers and sisters, that none of you has a sinful, unbelieving heart that turns away from the living God. But encourage one another daily, as long as it is called "Today," so that none of you may be hardened by sin's deceitfulness. We have come to share in Christ, if indeed we hold our original conviction firmly to the very end. As has just been said: "Today, if you hear his voice, do not harden your hearts as you did in the rebellion." … So we see that they were not able to enter, because of their unbelief.

Hebrews 5:11–14; 6:1–12: We have much to say about this, but it is hard to make it clear to you because you no longer try to understand. In fact, though by this time you ought to be teachers, you need someone to teach you the elementary truths of God's word all over again. You need milk, not solid food! Anyone who lives on milk, being still an infant, is not acquainted with the teaching about righteousness. But solid food is for the mature, who by constant use have trained themselves to distinguish good from evil … Therefore let us move beyond the elementary teachings about Christ and be taken forward to maturity, not laying again the foundation of repentance from acts that lead to death, and of faith in God, instruction about cleansing rites, the laying on of hands, the resurrection of the dead, and eternal judgment. And God permitting, we will do so. It is impossible for those who have once been enlightened, who have tasted the heavenly gift, who have shared in the Holy Spirit, who have tasted the goodness of the word of God and the powers of the coming age and who have fallen away, to be brought back to repentance. To their loss they are crucifying the Son of God all over again and subjecting him to public disgrace. Land that drinks in the rain often falling on it and that produces a crop useful to those for whom it is farmed receives the blessing of God. But land that produces thorns and thistles is worthless and is in danger of being cursed. In the end it will be burned. Even though we speak like this, dear friends, we are convinced of better things in your case—the things that have to do with salvation. God is not unjust; he will not forget your work and the love you have shown him as you have helped his people and continue to help them. We want each of you to show this same diligence to the very end, so that what you hope for may be fully realized. We do not want you to become lazy, but to imitate those who through faith and patience inherit what has been promised.

Hebrews 9:1–10: Now the first covenant had regulations for worship and also an earthly sanctuary. A tabernacle was set up. In its first room were the lampstand and the table with its consecrated bread; this was called the Holy Place. Behind the second curtain was a room called the Most Holy Place, which had the golden altar of incense and the gold-covered ark of the covenant. This ark contained the gold jar of manna, Aaron's staff that had budded, and the stone tablets of the covenant. Above the ark were the cherubim of the Glory, overshadowing the atonement cover. But we cannot discuss these things in detail now. When everything had been arranged like this, the priests entered regularly into the outer room to carry on their ministry. But only the high priest entered the inner room, and that only once a year, and never without blood, which he offered for himself and for the sins the people had committed in ignorance. The Holy Spirit was showing by this that the way into the Most Holy Place had not yet been disclosed as long as the first tabernacle was still functioning. This is an illustration for the present time, indicating that the gifts and sacrifices being offered were not able to clear the conscience of the worshiper. They are only a matter of food and drink and various ceremonial washings—external regulations applying until the time of the new order.

Hebrews 9:11–15: But when Christ came as high priest of the good things that are now already here, he went through the greater and more perfect tabernacle that is not made with human hands, that is to say, is not a part of this creation. He did not enter by means of the blood of goats and calves; but he entered the Most Holy Place once for all by his own blood, thus obtaining eternal redemption. The blood of goats and bulls and the ashes of a heifer sprinkled on those who are ceremonially unclean sanctify them so that they are outwardly clean. How much more, then, will the blood of Christ, who through the eternal Spirit offered himself unblemished to God, cleanse our consciences from acts that lead to death, so that we may serve the living God! For this reason Christ is the mediator of a new covenant, that those who are called may receive the promised eternal inheritance—now that he has died as a ransom to set them free from the sins committed under the first covenant.

Hebrews 10:1–18: The law is only a shadow of the good things that are coming—not the realities themselves. For this reason it can never, by the same sacrifices repeated endlessly year after year, make perfect those who draw near to worship. Otherwise, would they not have stopped being offered? For the worshipers would have been cleansed once for all, and would no longer have felt guilty for their sins. But those sacrifices are an annual reminder of sins. It is impossible for the blood of bulls and goats to take away sins. Therefore, when Christ came into the world, he said: "Sacrifice and offering you did not desire, but a body you prepared for me; with burnt offerings and sin offerings you were not pleased. Then I said, 'Here I am—it is written about me in the scroll—I have come to do your will, my God.'" First he said, "Sacrifices and offerings, burnt offerings and sin offerings you did not desire, nor were you pleased with them"—though they were offered in accordance with the law. Then he said, "Here I am, I have come to do your will." He sets aside the first to establish the second. And by that will, we have been made holy through the sacrifice of the body of Jesus Christ once for all. Day after day every priest stands and performs his religious duties; again and again he offers the same sacrifices, which can never take away sins. But when this priest had offered for all time one sacrifice for sins, he sat down at the right hand of God, and since that time he waits for his enemies to be made his footstool. For by one sacrifice he has made perfect forever those who are being made holy. The Holy Spirit also testifies to us about this. First he says: "This is the covenant I will make with them after that time, says the Lord. I will put my laws in their hearts, and I will write them on their minds." Then he adds: "Their sins and lawless acts I will remember no more." And where these have been forgiven, sacrifice for sin is no longer necessary.

Hebrews 10:19–39: Therefore, brothers and sisters, since we have confidence to enter the Most Holy Place by the blood of Jesus, by a new and living way opened for us through the curtain, that is, his body, and since we have a great priest over the house of God, let us draw near to God with a sincere heart and with the full assurance that faith brings, having our hearts sprinkled to cleanse us from a guilty conscience and having our bodies washed with pure water. Let us hold unswervingly to the hope we profess, for he who promised is faithful. And let us consider how we may spur one another on toward love and good deeds, not giving up meeting together, as some are in the habit of doing, but encouraging one another—and all the more as you see the Day approaching. If we deliberately keep on sinning after we have received the knowledge of the truth, no sacrifice for sins is left, but only a fearful expectation of judgment and of raging fire that will consume the enemies of God. Anyone who rejected the law of Moses died without mercy on the testimony of two or three witnesses. How much more severely do you think someone deserves to be punished who has trampled the Son of God underfoot, who has treated as an unholy thing the blood of the covenant that sanctified them, and who has insulted the Spirit of grace? For we know him who said, "It is mine to avenge; I will repay," and again, "The Lord will judge his people." It is a dreadful thing to fall into the hands of the living God. Remember those earlier days after you had received the light, when you endured in a great conflict full of suffering. Sometimes you were publicly exposed to insult and persecution; at other times you stood side by side with those who were so treated. You suffered along with those in prison and joyfully accepted the confiscation of your property, because you knew that you yourselves had better and lasting possessions. So do not throw away your confidence; it will be richly rewarded. You need to persevere so that when you have done the will of God, you will receive what he has promised. For, "In just a little while, he who is coming will come and will not delay." "But my righteous one will live by faith. And I take no pleasure in the one who shrinks back." But we do not belong to those who shrink back and are destroyed, but to those who have faith and are saved.

1 Peter 1:1–2: Peter, an apostle of Jesus Christ, To God's elect, exiles scattered throughout the provinces of Pontus, Galatia, Cappadocia, Asia and Bithynia, who have been chosen according to the foreknowledge of God the Father, through the sanctifying work of the Spirit, to be obedient to Jesus Christ and sprinkled with his blood: Grace and peace be yours in abundance.

1 Peter 1:3–12: Praise be to the God and Father of our Lord Jesus Christ! In his great mercy he has given us new birth into a living hope through the resurrection of Jesus Christ from the dead, and into an inheritance that can never perish, spoil or fade. This inheritance is kept in heaven for you, who through faith are shielded by God's power until the coming of the salvation that is ready to be revealed in the last time. In all this you greatly rejoice, though now for a little while you may have had to suffer grief in all kinds of trials. These have come so that the proven genuineness of your faith—of greater worth than gold, which perishes even though refined by fire—may result in praise, glory and honor when Jesus Christ is revealed. Though you have not seen him, you love him; and even though you do not see him now, you believe in him and are filled with an inexpressible and glorious joy, for you are receiving the end result of your faith, the salvation of your souls. Concerning this salvation, the prophets, who spoke of the grace that was to come to you, searched intently and with the greatest care, trying to find out the time and circumstances to which the Spirit of Christ in them was pointing when he predicted the sufferings of the Messiah and the glories that would follow. It was revealed to them that they were not serving themselves but you, when they spoke of the things that have now been told you by those who have preached the gospel to you by the Holy Spirit sent from heaven. Even angels long to look into these things.

1 Peter 3:15–22: But in your hearts revere Christ as Lord. Always be prepared to give an answer to everyone who asks you to give the reason for the hope that you have. But do this with gentleness and respect, keeping a clear conscience, so that those who speak maliciously against your good behavior in Christ may be ashamed of their slander. For it is better, if it is God's will, to suffer for doing good than for doing evil. For Christ also suffered once for sins, the righteous for the unrighteous, to bring you to God. He was put to death in the body but made alive in the Spirit. After being made alive, he went and made proclamation to the imprisoned spirits— to those who were disobedient long ago when God waited patiently in the days of Noah while the ark was being built. In it only a few people, eight in all, were saved through water, and this water symbolizes baptism that now saves you also—not the removal of dirt from the body but the pledge of a clear conscience toward God. It saves you by the resurrection of Jesus Christ, who has gone into heaven and is at God's right hand—with angels, authorities and powers in submission to him.

1 Peter 4:1–7: Therefore, since Christ suffered in his body, arm yourselves also with the same attitude, because whoever suffers in the body is done with sin. As a result, they do not live the rest of their earthly lives for evil human desires, but rather for the will of God. For you have spent enough time in the past doing what pagans choose to do—living in debauchery, lust, drunkenness, orgies, carousing and detestable idolatry. They are surprised that you do not join them in their reckless, wild living, and they heap abuse on you. But they will have to give account to him who is ready to judge the living and the dead. For this is the reason the gospel was preached even to those who are now dead, so that they might be judged according to human standards in regard to the body, but live according to God in regard to the Spirit. The end of all things is near. Therefore be alert and of sober mind so that you may pray.

1 Peter 4:12–19: Dear friends, do not be surprised at the fiery ordeal that has come on you to test you, as though something strange were happening to you. But rejoice inasmuch as you participate in the sufferings of Christ, so that you may be overjoyed when his glory is revealed. If you are insulted because of the name of Christ, you are blessed, for the Spirit of glory and of God rests on you. If you suffer, it should not be as a murderer or thief or any other kind of criminal, or even as a meddler. However, if you suffer as a Christian, do not be ashamed, but praise God that you bear that name. For it is time for judgment to begin with God's household; and if it begins with us, what will the outcome be for those who do not obey the gospel of God? And, "If it is hard for the righteous to be saved, what will become of the ungodly and the sinner?" So then, those who suffer according to God's will should commit themselves to their faithful Creator and continue to do good.

2 Peter 1:12–21: So I will always remind you of these things, even though you know them and are firmly established in the truth you now have. I think it is right to refresh your memory as long as I live in the tent of this body, because I know that I will soon put it aside, as our Lord Jesus Christ has made clear to me. And I will make every effort to see that after my departure you will always be able to remember these things. For we did not follow cleverly devised stories when we told you about the coming of our Lord Jesus Christ in power, but we were eyewitnesses of his majesty. He received honor and glory from God the Father when the voice came to him from the Majestic Glory, saying, "This is my Son, whom I love; with him I am well pleased." We ourselves heard this voice that came from heaven when we were with him on the sacred mountain. We also have the prophetic message as something completely reliable, and you will do well to pay attention to it, as to a light shining in a dark place, until the day dawns and the morning star rises in your hearts. Above all, you must understand that no prophecy of Scripture came about by the prophet's own interpretation of things. For prophecy never had its origin in the human will, but prophets, though human, spoke from God as they were carried along by the Holy Spirit.

1 John 2:18–25: Dear children, this is the last hour; and as you have heard that the antichrist is coming, even now many antichrists have come. This is how we know it is the last hour. They went out from us, but they did not really belong to us. For if they had belonged to us, they would have remained with us; but their going showed that none of them belonged to us. But you have an anointing from the Holy One, and all of you know the truth. I do not write to you because you do not know the truth, but because you do know it and because no lie comes from the truth. Who is the liar? It is whoever denies that Jesus is the Christ. Such a person is the antichrist—denying the Father and the Son. No one who denies the

Son has the Father; whoever acknowledges the Son has the Father also. As for you, see that what you have heard from the beginning remains in you. If it does, you also will remain in the Son and in the Father. And this is what he promised us—eternal life. [Note: "But you have an anointing from the Holy One, and *all* of you know the truth" confirms universal anointing—not a special anointing of exclusivity (emphasis mine).]

1 John 3:19–24: This is how we know that we belong to the truth and how we set our hearts at rest in his presence: If our hearts condemn us, we know that God is greater than our hearts, and he knows everything. Dear friends, if our hearts do not condemn us, we have confidence before God and receive from him anything we ask, because we keep his commands and do what pleases him. And this is his command: to believe in the name of his Son, Jesus Christ, and to love one another as he commanded us. The one who keeps God's commands lives in him, and he in them. And this is how we know that he lives in us: We know it by the Spirit he gave us. (Note: "We know it by the Spirit he gave *us*" indicates that this giving is all-inclusive throughout the redeemed—the body of Christ. (emphasis mine).]

1 John 4:1–6: Dear friends, do not believe every spirit, but test the spirits to see whether they are from God, because many false prophets have gone out into the world. This is how you can recognize the Spirit of God: Every spirit that acknowledges that Jesus Christ has come in the flesh is from God, but every spirit that does not acknowledge Jesus is not from God. This is the spirit of the antichrist, which you have heard is coming and even now is already in the world. You, dear children, are from God and have overcome them, because the one who is in you is greater than the one who is in the world. They are from the world and therefore speak from the viewpoint of the world, and the world listens to them. We are from God, and whoever knows God listens to us; but whoever is not from God does not listen to us. This is how we recognize the Spirit of truth and the spirit of falsehood.

1 John 4:7–21: Dear friends, let us love one another, for love comes from God. Everyone who loves has been born of God and knows God. Whoever does not love does not know God, because God is love. This is how God showed his love among us: He sent his one and only Son into the world that we might live through him. This is love: not that we loved God, but that he loved us and sent his Son as an atoning sacrifice for our sins. Dear friends, since God so loved us, we also ought to love one another. No one has ever seen God; but if we love one another, God lives in us and his love is made complete in us. This is how we know that we live in him and he in us: He has given us of his Spirit. And we have seen and testify that the Father has sent his Son to be the Savior of the world. If anyone acknowledges that Jesus is the Son of God, God lives in them and they in God. And so we know and rely on the love God has for us. God is love. Whoever lives in love lives in God, and God in them. This is how love is made complete among us so that we will have confidence on the day of judgment: In this world we are like Jesus. There is no fear in love. But perfect love drives out fear, because fear has to do with punishment. The one who fears is not made perfect in love. We love because he first loved us. Whoever claims to love God yet hates a brother or sister is a liar. For whoever does not love their brother and sister, whom they have seen, cannot love God, whom they have not seen. And he has given us this command: Anyone who loves God must also love their brother and sister.

1 John 5:1–12: Everyone who believes that Jesus is the Christ is born of God, and everyone who loves the father loves his child as well. This is how we know that we love the children of God: by loving God and carrying out his commands. In fact, this is love for God: to keep his commands. And his commands are not burdensome, for everyone born of God overcomes the world. This is the victory that has overcome the world, even our faith. Who is it that overcomes the world? Only the one who believes that Jesus is the Son of God. This is the one who came by water and blood—Jesus Christ. He did not come by water only, but by water and blood.

And it is the Spirit who testifies, because the Spirit is the truth. For there are three that testify: the Spirit, the water and the blood; and the three are in agreement. We accept human testimony, but God's testimony is greater because it is the testimony of God, which he has given about his Son. Whoever believes in the Son of God accepts this testimony. Whoever does not believe God has made him out to be a liar, because they have not believed the testimony God has given about his Son. And this is the testimony: God has given us eternal life, and this life is in his Son. Whoever has the Son has life; whoever does not have the Son of God does not have life.

Jude 17–25: But, dear friends, remember what the apostles of our Lord Jesus Christ foretold. They said to you, "In the last times there will be scoffers who will follow their own ungodly desires." These are the people who divide you, who follow mere natural instincts and do not have the Spirit. But you, dear friends, by building yourselves up in your most holy faith and praying in the Holy Spirit, keep yourselves in God's love as you wait for the mercy of our Lord Jesus Christ to bring you to eternal life. Be merciful to those who doubt; save others by snatching them from the fire; to others show mercy, mixed with fear—hating even the clothing stained by corrupted flesh. To him who is able to keep you from stumbling and to present you before his glorious presence without fault and with great joy—to the only God our Savior be glory, majesty, power and authority, through Jesus Christ our Lord, before all ages, now and forevermore! Amen. [Note: This is confirmation of the all-inclusive indwelling Holy Spirit. Each and every soul redeemed by Jesus's precious blood is permanently indwelled by the Holy Spirit.]

Revelation 1:9–11: I, John, your brother and companion in the suffering and kingdom and patient endurance that are ours in Jesus, was on the island of Patmos because of the word of God and the testimony of Jesus. On the Lord's Day I was in the Spirit, and I heard behind me a loud voice like a trumpet, which said: "Write on a scroll what you see and send it to the seven churches: to Ephesus, Smyrna, Pergamum, Thyatira, Sardis, Philadelphia and Laodicea."

Revelation 2:7: Whoever has ears, let them hear what the Spirit says to the churches. To the one who is victorious, I will give the right to eat from the tree of life, which is in the paradise of God.

Revelation 2:11: Whoever has ears, let them hear what the Spirit says to the churches. The one who is victorious will not be hurt at all by the second death.

Revelation 2:17: Whoever has ears, let them hear what the Spirit says to the churches. To the one who is victorious, I will give some of the hidden manna. I will also give that person a white stone with a new name written on it, known only to the one who receives it.

Revelation 2:26–29: To the one who is victorious and does my will to the end, I will give authority over the nations— that one "will rule them with an iron scepter and will dash them to pieces like pottery" —just as I have received authority from my Father I will also give that one the morning star. Whoever has ears, let them hear what the Spirit says to the churches.

Revelation 3:5–6: The one who is victorious will, like them, be dressed in white. I will never blot out the name of that person from the book of life, but will acknowledge that name before my Father and his angels. Whoever has ears, let them hear what the Spirit says to the churches.

Revelation 3:12–13: The one who is victorious I will make a pillar in the temple of my God. Never again will they leave it. I will write on them the name of my God and the name of the city of my God, the new Jerusalem, which is coming down out of heaven from my God; and I will also write on them my new name. Whoever has ears, let them hear what the Spirit says to the churches.

Revelation 3:21–22: To the one who is victorious, I will give the right to sit with me on my throne, just as I was victorious and sat down with my Father on his throne. Whoever has ears, let them hear what the Spirit says to the churches.

Revelation 4:1–3: After this I looked, and there before me was a door standing open in heaven. And the voice I had first heard speaking to me like a trumpet said, "Come up here, and I will show you what must take place after this." At once I was in the Spirit, and there before me was a throne in heaven with someone sitting on it. And the one who sat there had the appearance of jasper and ruby. A rainbow that shone like an emerald encircled the throne.

Revelation 11:11: But after the three and a half days the breath of life from God entered them, and they stood on their feet, and terror struck those who saw them. [Note: "The breath of life"—the Holy Spirit—is here. See chapter 11:1–14 for the full picture.]

Revelation 14:13: Then I heard a voice from heaven say, "Write this: Blessed are the dead who die in the Lord from now on." "Yes," says the Spirit, "they will rest from their labor, for their deeds will follow them."

Revelation 17:3: Then the angel carried me away in the Spirit into a wilderness. There I saw a woman sitting on a scarlet beast that was covered with blasphemous names and had seven heads and ten horns.

Revelation 19:10: At this I fell at his feet to worship him. But he said to me, "Don't do that! I am a fellow servant with you and with your brothers and sisters who hold to the testimony of Jesus. Worship God! For it is the Spirit of prophecy who bears testimony to Jesus."

Revelation 21:9–10: One of the seven angels who had the seven bowls full of the seven last plagues came and said to me, "Come, I will show you the bride, the wife of the Lamb." And he carried me away in the Spirit to a mountain great and high, and showed me the Holy City, Jerusalem, coming down out of heaven from God.

Revelation 22:17: The Spirit and the bride say, "Come!" And let the one who hears say, "Come!" Let the one who is thirsty come; and let the one who wishes take the free gift of the water of life.

Printed in the United States
By Bookmasters